A LIFE IN DEATH

A LIFE IN DEATH

RICHARD VENABLES, QPM

WITH KRIS HOLLINGTON

THISTLE
PUBLISHING

"The care with which our dead are treated is a mark of how civilised a society we are. Much goes on for understandable reasons behind closed doors. For this reason there is a special responsibility placed on those entrusted with this work and the authorities who supervise it to ensure that the bodies of the dead are treated with the utmost care and respect. That is what bereaved and loved ones are entitled to expect and what society at large demands."

Charles Haddon-Cave, QC

"Disaster Victim Identification is the internationally-accepted term to describe the procedures for recovering and identifying deceased victims and human remains from mass fatality incidents and of the support given to family and friends during the identification process."

The College of Policing Authorised
Professional Practice

"At the worst time of their lives, we owe it to them, as professionals, to do our very best"

I have always tried to live up to this police maxim in my work and I can only hope that I have succeeded. With this in mind, *A Life in Death* is dedicated to all deceased victims of major disasters and to those who loved them in life.

And, for so many reasons, this book is also dedicated to Mum and Dad.

ONE

PROLOGUE

I had lived with the stench of death for years but had never experienced anything like this.

Fifteen hours after leaving the UK in the grip of midwinter I was standing on the banks of a muddy blood-red river looking through heat waves at a devastated landscape. There was no birdsong, only the buzzing of flies and the occasional barking of dogs. And there was the smell: death and raw sewerage, thick as fog.

Along the riverbanks were dozens of metal freight containers about the size and height of a large bedroom.

We had driven for two-and-half hours from the airport and watched as paradise transformed into hell. Beachside villas, bars and clubs, white sands and palm trees that had once drawn so many visitors, were all gone. Anything that hadn't been swept away was in ruins and covered in drying mud and debris.

9.3 on the Richter scale. The third largest earthquake in recorded history had lasted for ten minutes and unleashed enough power (the equivalent of 230,000 Hiroshimas) to shift the planet almost half an inch on its axis. Around 250,000 people were dead. One third of them were children, easily overcome by the surging water.

Our destination was Wat Yan Yao, a Buddhist temple on Thailand's southwest peninsula. With hundreds and then thousands of bodies being recovered, temples were being used as temporary mortuaries. With no electricity or running water, they were hardly ideal but there was simply nowhere better to take them.

The moment we emerged from the sanctuary of the air-conditioned Land Cruiser the smell hit us like a mallet. If you can imagine an overheated warehouse that's been storing putrefied meat, rotting vegetables and raw sewerage for several weeks then you're halfway there. There was no escape, it didn't matter if you were indoors or out, there was no choice but to breathe it in and get used to it.

Once we'd donned our protective gear (white coveralls, gumboots, gloves and masks), I led the way in through the ornate gateway that took us into the grounds. The main temple building was ahead of us. It was sixty feet tall and its red, gold and blue polished stone façade glowed in the evening sun.

Monks were praying for the dead while men laid blocks of dry ice around dozens of newly-recovered bodies that were yet to be placed in body bags.

The bodies, shrouded in the dry ice's spectral white mist, were all golden brown, discoloured by sun and mud and swollen by bacteria; it was obvious they would be unrecognizable even to their closest relatives. I couldn't even tell if they were Asian or European.

The 'mortuary' consisted of a few tents and a couple of porta cabins, also with no power or running water, which served as makeshift body storage units. After completing my inspection I walked down to the river, to the main storage units.

"Are you sure you want to see this?" my Thai guide asked. "The army only went near here wearing breathing apparatus."

I had to. If I was going to have any chance of sorting this out, then I needed to know what we were dealing with. Just recovering bodies was proving to be a mammoth task for a police force already stretched to the limit rescuing injured survivors. A total of 3,600 corpses from the popular tourist resort of Khao Lak Beach alone found their way to the temple at Wat Yan Yao in the first three days after the disaster. The fact that these victims, who had died in salt water and had been placed in metal boxes in 35C heat some days earlier already gave me a good idea of what we were up against. But I had to get it out of my system. See it, breathe it in, get used to it and crack on. We were in a race against time with fast-spreading, old-school diseases: cholera, typhoid, diphtheria and dysentery.

I braced myself as my guide, wearing a mask, unbolted the metal door and it clanged back.

"So," the guide said. "We think there are about 5,000 so far. Where do you want to begin?

TWO

BAPTISM OF FIRE

I was climbing through the upstairs bedroom window of an ordinary-looking, smart little detached house in Mexborough when I caught the unmistakable scent of death. It was August 1988 and I was a 31-year-old CID detective sergeant assigned to a murder squad trying to jail a mass murderer. I paused and took another breath. Yes, not overpowering but definitely there.

Mick, a solid and trustworthy detective, followed me through the window a moment later. We exchanged a look, knowing in some sense what was to come. The bedroom had been ransacked; clothes were strewn about, furniture had been jostled or overturned.

A dog barked. It hadn't made a sound when we'd knocked at the door. It stayed downstairs, possibly guarding the dead body of its owner, while we checked the upstairs, moving more slowly than normal, not wanting to shock ourselves. All clear, until I reached the bathroom. The toilet was stuffed full of neckties. I caught my reflection in the bathroom mirror. My skin was pale grey and I looked terrified.

Mick's pallor and expression matched mine.

Dry mouthed, hearts pounding, we started to make our way downstairs. I was closest to the bannister with Mick on the walled side of staircase.

I tried to get some moisture in my throat. I could barely get the words out.

"You know what we're going to find down there, don't you Mick?"

Mick swallowed.

"Yes sarge."

We paused halfway down, and I kid you not, we held hands like a pair of kids from Scooby Doo. I had, in my twelve years of policing, seen dozens of dead bodies in states unimaginable to most people (even other cops), and our prime suspect was already in custody.

So why was I so bloody scared?

***

Twelve years earlier, in May 1976, as part of my initial training as an 18-and-a-half-year-old police constable for South Yorkshire Police, I was taken with five other fresh-faced, newly crew-cutted recruits on a visit to a mortuary to view an autopsy. You didn't have to stay for the whole thing but you did have to at least see a body.

Our sergeant waved us off with a big grin. We were in for a "treat", apparently. My first surprise was to see that the senior forensic pathologist that day was Professor Alan Usher. Just a few weeks earlier he'd held my balls in his hand as part of the police medical. Now I was going to see those same hands elbow-deep in a corpse.

I hadn't been able to sleep the previous night. The thought of going to the mortuary had really unnerved me but I was reassured by the sedate introduction given by an attendant who described the correct way to store a body and then the autopsy process, including continuity and paperwork. Then he handed us our aprons and plastic overshoes.

'Oh well,' I thought, as I fumbled to get the apron over my uniform, 'No turning back now.'

Professor Usher then told us the history of the person we were going to see.

"This is a 35-year-old male, a resident at Middlewood Mental Hospital. He'd been missing for about three weeks when he was found trapped in one of the heating ducts. He'd tried to escape but became stuck and died there."

The Professor paused for a moment.

"Some of you might not like what you're going to see."

We entered the autopsy room. We all flinched as the cloying smell of putrefaction hit our noses like a right hook. The body was covered in a white sheet, which only worsened our apprehension. When it was lifted back, however, I found the sight so surprising that I forgot for a moment what we were looking at.

He was green and swollen. The skin, stretched smooth, looked like solidified jelly and I thought the colour was remarkably similar to that of the Incredible Hulk or the Jolly Green Giant. He only resembled a human in the vaguest terms. He was covered in white maggots, the sort I'd used for fishing when a young lad. They swarmed in his eye sockets and mouth. For me, the smell was worse than the sight and I watched with interest as Professor Usher began the autopsy and started to lecture us on everything we might want to know about dead bodies.

"There are five main stages in the process of human decomposition, summarised using the acronym FBAAD: Fresh, Bloat, Active, Advanced, and Dry. Stage one, or fresh decomposition, occurs in the hours immediately after death, as blood coalesces in veins and muscles, the result of a stilled heart. We'd expect to see dark blue or black hands and feet in a hanging victim, for example, wherever the blood has collected. Autolysis follows; decay leads to the release of cellular enzymes into body cells and muscular tissue, and this gets the process of decomposition properly. As oxygen disappears, anaerobic organisms start to turn proteins and lipids – molecules containing fats, vitamins, and waxes – of the body's fresh and organs – into hydrogen sulphide and methane, along with other acids and gases which brings us into stage two as these gases lead to bloating of the body. Then, as we reach stage three, maggots appear and fluids flow out as tissues liquefy. Then we reach the Advanced stage of decay, most material has broken down, being absorbed by the surrounding earth – if lying on the ground or buried – leading to the creation of a corpse decomposition island, a stained area of ground that contains more carbon and nitrogen than the surrounding area. If left on the ground, plants will spring up, absorbing the excess calcium, phosphorus, and magnesium and the area will be richer in plant life than areas nearby. Stage five is skeletonisation. Generally, bones will survive nearly all conditions if buried but factors like temperature, oxygen levels in the soil, not forgetting moisture and pH balance are just four variables that can lead to the disintegration or redistribution, absorption into wet soil and moved by river or tidal lagoon, for example. Here we have reached the stage of decomposition were saponification is taking place."

I asked what that was.

"The remaining tissue is turned into adipocere, known as grave wax. The fatter the person, the sooner this happens. It also happens where decomposition agents are absent, as in this case. This wax, usually brownish white, falls off the body fairly quickly."

I asked a few more questions and I became conscious at some point that I was the only one of my group talking. I turned. No one was there; the door to the autopsy room was just swinging shut, the result of a stampede to the toilet.

Professor Usher, meanwhile, was professional and enthusiastic and I became really absorbed by the whole process.

"Don't worry," the pathologist told the group at the end of the visit, some of whom were still looking quite poorly. "That was a real baptism of fire. You'll never see anything like that again in your entire career."

***

Although I was nearly nineteen, I looked closer to fifteen. People looked at my uniform disbelievingly and asked me if I'd started shaving yet. I was definitely naive, like all teenagers, and the job kept me on my toes. I learned an important lesson during the first month of my beat, when I received a phone call from the neighbour of an old woman who lived alone.

"I haven't seen her for three days," she said. "Her curtains have been closed and she's not taken in the milk."

I duly prepared the neighbours and family for the worst and said I would try and gain access as no one held a spare key. When I arrived at the house the keys were in the lock on the inside, so I used my truncheon to break the smallest window and I slowly reached in and turned the mortise.

I shouted the old girl's name and I checked each room before going upstairs. She was in bed, blankets neatly placed over her chest. She looked peaceful. 'Gone quietly, at least,' I thought and, as we'd been taught, I leaned over to confirm she was dead and placed my finger on her jugular to feel for a pulse.

The subsequent ear-splitting scream that followed confirmed that my diagnosis was entirely incorrect.

"What the hell are you doing in my house?" she demanded as I tried to stop my heart bouncing around in my chest like a rubber ball.

"You neighbour called, she hasn't seen you for days, the milk's out," I explained breathlessly, clutching my heart with my right hand.

"I was feeling a bit poorly so stayed in bed," she said before remarking I was the first man in her bedroom since her late husband.

We had a cuppa after I'd given the family and neighbours the good news.

This lesson (don't believe your eyes and/or looks can be deceiving) was soon followed by my first real death, and this also contained a number of important and unforgettable lessons. The first was that the human body is bloody heavy and deceased bodies are incredibly difficult to manoeuvre. The man in question was the landlord of a local pub. He'd been found dead in bed. Fine so far. But when I saw him, well, he was the size and girth of Giant Haystacks. He must have weighed between seventeen and twenty stone. Four undertakers turned up but it wasn't enough. It took six of us to steer him down the winding stairs, which was made even more difficult by the fact that we weren't able to get him on a stretcher, a somewhat undignified removal to say the least, and we were all sweating and nursing pulled muscles by the time the body was finally straining the suspension of the mortuary vehicle.

My next lesson came when I had to tag the body with a label tied to his right toe. This was the first time I'd touched the skin of a dead body. We didn't bother with gloves in those days and I struggled to maintain my professionalism (I didn't want my colleagues to think I was a wimp) as I fumbled to get the label and string tied on. The most unnerving part for me was the lack of warmth. Touching another human being is usually a warming experience. It felt so totally alien and I wasn't prepared for the coldness.

Job done, I looked down at the body. I knew then that I didn't like dealing with deaths but, as I learned, dealing with a dead body was unpleasant, but that was nothing when compared to the other aspect of death – the loved ones they leave behind.

One afternoon I mentioned to my sarge that I hadn't dealt with a road traffic accident (new recruits are expected to deal with a wide range of incidents to gain experience, especially if they want promotion).

A few minutes later, at 5:20pm a report came in of an RTA and the sarge said: "Whatever it is, it's yours Venables."

Small Renault meets school bus head-on in a narrow country road. Several of the public-school pupils were injured, but not seriously (chief witness was thirteen-year-old William Hague, the future Conservative Foreign Secretary, who'd been a front seat passenger on the bus). The 51-year-old driver of the Renault was unconscious and seriously injured. She was a teacher from the local teacher training college and had skidded on one of the large patches of mud left on the wet road by various agricultural vehicles. She died on her way to hospital.

I went to the mortuary as part of the continuity, which meant I had to identify the body as the woman I had seen in the car upon my arrival at the scene. She was absolutely intact, not a mark on her, and her eyes were open. Mum had often said to me that "the eyes are the windows to your soul," and those words came back to me at that moment and I felt crushed. This was my first experience of seeing death like this; so powerful yet serene. My inspector asked me if I wanted to stay for the autopsy but I just couldn't. I later found out that she died from a lacerated liver.

The following morning was far, far worse. I went to see her husband and we sat in his kitchen. He couldn't speak, choked on tears every time he tried. Then the kids came out of the lounge. Four of them. Two of whom were eight-year-old twin boys who both started to bawl the moment they saw my uniform. The eldest daughter was in her late teens and she quickly guided the boys back to the lounge.

I was swept along with the husband's emotion. The grief was overwhelming and I just wasn't ready; I hadn't known what to expect but this was just too much. The husband was extremely dignified and I think pulled himself together for my sake; I wasn't much older than his eldest daughter.

When I got home, I couldn't get the kids out of my mind and, cried my eyes out and kept crying for a good while after. There was no counselling, no debrief. I, like every other cop dealing with similar situations back then, was just left to find my own way to cope.

I learned then that I would never make a good traffic cop. Dealing with road crashes like this was not for me. As my career progressed and I dealt with more accidents, more sudden deaths, my fear of the dead started to dissipate. Dead bodies were much easier to deal with than grieving families; a body is not going to spit or swear at me, ask awkward questions, or look at me in that heart-wrenching, "please bring them back" way. Whenever I had the option, I would say to a colleague: "I'll do the requirements around the body if you see the family."

Jennifer and I married in August 1978, aged 19 and 20 respectively. In July 1979, Jen was due to give birth and I was at work at 8.30am on the ninth when I got a message to say that she was being induced. This was immediately followed by an emergency call: a high-speed passenger train had hit someone in Swinton. That was my patch, there was no one to cover and it was an emergency, so I simply had to attend.

A team of engineers had been working on a fast stretch of line. A man had been posted to Swinton Bridge as look-out but even though he warned his colleagues, the train had been going too fast and the workers had to jump for their lives, and one of them wasn't quick enough. He was killed instantly.

While Sarah was being born (she arrived at 12.45pm) I was still picking body parts up of the tracks. There were no trained specialists in those days and it was left to whichever cops were there. And again, no welfare or counselling afterwards and once I finally made it to the hospital I was full of emotion, good and bad (this was my first experience of a disrupted body). I couldn't shake the thought that Jen had been creating life, through my beautiful daughter, Sarah, as this poor man lost his.

This experience reminded me of the story of my own birthday, a tale often repeated in my family. Wednesday 28 August 1957, at home: 39 Angel Street, Bolton-on-Dearne, a mining community near Rotherham in South Yorkshire. My screams failed to drown out Chopin's Piano Sonata No.2 coming from the chapel next door, where the rest of my family was saying goodbye to Grandmother Louisa, Dad's mum, who'd died a few days earlier.

Death was part of my life right from the start. Great Aunt Harriet worked on behalf of the local undertaker in Bolton-On-Dearne, being the first person to respond to a home death (she was paid per body). Auntie Harriet would go to the house, strip the body, wash it, re-clothe it and then place it on a body board, which she then – with some help – placed on two easels, ready for viewing by the family. She kept a 6-foot wooden body board, in the shape of a coffin lid, behind the pantry door of her terraced home.

Grandad David (Great Aunt Harriet's brother and Louisa's husband) introduced me to killing when I was about five years old. He worked his whole life at Barnburgh Colliery, retiring in 1965. He kept a large and immaculate prize-winning allotment (he grew champion roses) behind his terraced house. Far more fascinating to me than the roses and countless vegetables were the pigs, which Grandad raised from piglets until they were ready for market. I ran to see the pigs every time we visited and watched them grow up.

One day Grandad gave me a certain look, a tilt of the head, waiting 'til he had me fixed in his gaze.

"You should come down and watch."

"Watch what, Grandad?"

The mini slaughterhouse, a solid brick building about three metres long and two metres wide, stood in the rear yard of his house. White-washed walls, large concrete shelf built into one wall, stainless steel sink at the far end with a single copper tap. Empty apart from a series of hooks bolted to a wooden ceiling beam.

My older brothers, Robert and Michael, weren't interested in Grandad's pigs but I felt privileged that Grandad (with Dad's blessing) had asked me into this secret, adult place that fine, warm summer morning.

Grandad left me with Dad for a moment while he nipped into his shed. He came out with a satchel and peering inside, I saw the silver flash of steel. He set about sharpening and the three of us sat in the sun for a while, chatting about this and that, school and family, as Grandad carefully, steadily, expertly – *precisely* – sharpened each implement.

I felt a bit nervous when Grandad finished and brought up the first pig.

My eyes saucered when Grandad took a captive bolt gun out of his jacket pocket. I thought it was a real revolver and couldn't wait to tell my schoolmates that my Grandad had a gun, just like a detective.

Grandad maneuvered the pig so that he was square on.

"I'm just going to stun the pig now," he said quietly. "That way it will feel no pain."

Grandad took hold of the pig's ears and gently steadied its head. He placed the barrel between the pig's eyes.

The pig seemed agitated. Did it know what was coming, just as a human would?

A solid bang, not as loud as a gunshot, but loud enough in that little space. The pig jerked and its legs gave way.

"To get the best meat," Grandad said, speaking more loudly now, "The pig needs bleeding."

He quickly slit its throat, ear-to-ear. I was not frightened. I felt no emotion for the pig. This was how men turned an animal into food. It was a process.

There was so much blood. Dark and thick. Once it had stopped flowing, Grandad swished some of it away with a bucket of water. Dad helped Grandad lift the pig onto the concrete slab, both of them groaning and cursing with the effort. Using hot water and sharp knives they shaved the pig of hair. Grandad then took a large knife and stabbed and sawed at the under-belly, and then eviscerated the animal, telling me which organ was what before carefully putting each onto the concrete slab next to the pig. He was enjoying himself and it was infectious. When I saw the huge, never-ending intestines, I thought they were ready-made sausages.

Eventually, Dad and Grandad lifted the gutted pig and hooked it under the beam. Job done. From that day on, I decided, I would join Grandad for the slaughter and these experiences stood me in great stead on the day of my first autopsy viewing (if such an event had taken place these days, I suspect Grandad would have been arrested for child cruelty).

* * *

So, after all the death I'd experienced in my young life, why was I so bloody scared on that staircase? Because this person had been murdered. I had never discovered a murdered body before. And we knew that the killer, 22-year-old Anthony Arkwright, who was at that moment being grilled by experienced CID detectives, was an exceptionally savage killer. He had murdered his 45-year-old neighbour, ex-teacher Raymond Ford, stabbing him 250 times before disembowelling the corpse and draping his entrails around the room, scattering some of his internal organs in the hallway. Marcus Law, an acquaintance of Arkwright, in a wheelchair after a motorbike accident, was stabbed seventy times, and left with cigarettes stuffed in his mouth and ears, his eyes gouged out, cigarettes left in the sockets. Arkwright said it was revenge for all the cigarettes Law had scrounged.

I was nearest the hallway and so turned to lean over the bannister and look back down the hallway. I could see her through the open kitchen doorway. Arkwright's grandmother was lying on the floor. An axe was buried in her head.

"Mick," I said hoarsely, "She's dead and it's not a pretty sight."

Mick's eyes were as wide as an owl's. We were eight stairs from the hallway and we stayed put as the shock settled in and then, as is so often the case, our training kicked in. Preserve the scene. I descended the stairs, approached the body. No need to check if she was dead, so no need to contaminate the scene any more. We turned and left by the front door. As I opened it I was confronted by the sight of Arkwright's brother on the front path, next to the ladder we'd used to climb in. Now I had to tell him his grandmother had been murdered. I had no time to think about phrasing and blurted it out, quickly closing the door behind me, so there was no chance he would see.

Next job was to call the incident room. I spoke to the senior investigating officer Derek Smith who was in a celebratory mood as Arkwright had been charged with the two murders. I told him that there was a third victim; that no one had seen Arkwright's Grandad for a couple of days and, from talking to a neighbour who'd said he'd heard the family's other dog barking from inside the allotment shed, I thought we needed to check it out.

"Fuck off Dick, you're having a laugh, go and enjoy your weekend, you've been working some long hours."

Once I'd persuaded him I was telling the truth, we travelled to the allotment shed where we could hear the dog barking. We broke in and found Grandad, killed by blows to the head with a lump hammer.

As I'd discovered both bodies, I had to attend both autopsies for continuity, to confirm my identification and then to relate any new information to the enquiry team immediately after.

When I spoke to one of the case officers he said: "Arkwright asked for a deck of cards. So we brought him one. He cut the pack, revealing the four of hearts. He said 'That's how I decided how many I would kill.' Thank god he didn't draw a ten."

I'd been on duty 23hours by the time I got home for a terrible round of nightmare-filled sleep. This was another valuable lesson. I had previously dismissed the trauma people said they suffer from the discovery of dead bodies, especially murder victims. The victims came alive again in my dreams, only to be murdered once more, leaving me awake and wide-eyed, sweating and entangled in the bedsheets.

THREE

WEDNESDAY'S CHILD

N ot long into my service, I was working the 6am to 2pm shift on Christmas Day. At 1.45pm, I was called to a domestic.

'There goes my Christmas dinner,' I thought.

I went to the address and was amazed to find that I recognised the accused as one of the kids who used to beat me up on my way home from school.

My application form had said I wanted to join the police to help people and to make a difference. In truth, I wanted to be a policeman because it would give me an identity. I would be a respected 'somebody' in the community (these were the days when cops commanded that kind of respect). I wanted the uniform; I wanted to be instantly recognisable. My enthusiasm gained even more momentum when, as a police cadet, my older brother Mike brought his girlfriend home. She was gorgeous and he made it clear that there were plenty of girls who loved cops. I'd not had much success with ladies. Sixteen and 5ft2", I was short for my age and had auburn hair. Being small and ginger meant I was the school bullies' ideal fodder.

After school was done with I wanted more than anything to join the police but I was six inches too short, eighteen months too young and although I managed seven O-levels, I only managed to scrape a CSE Grade 2 in maths – not good enough for the police. I went back to school with my self-esteem at an all-time low. My plan was to retake maths and do some A-Levels.

And then the miracle happened. I started to grow. My hair gradually turned brown. I wasn't bullied. I became a Prefect and earned respect. I made friends and was even invited to parties.

But I still had no luck with the ladies.

Then, for my seventeenth birthday I got a Lambretta GP 200 scooter. It had fourteen mirrors and two aerials and sounded like a washing machine on full spin filled with angry wasps.

"You know what mate," I told Noz, my best mate at the time, "This may just get me a girl!"

And it did – in October 1974 whilst visiting my local Chinese take away I met my first wife Jen, who was fifteen and obviously impressed by my 'circus wagon' (as Dad named it). We were engaged in 1976 and married two years later. We were very young, but in those days that was the only way to be together.

I was at last tall enough and educated enough but I still had nine months to go until I was old enough (you had to be 18-and-a-half) so found work as a chock-fitter with the National Coal Board working at Elsecar Central Workshops in Barnsley; hard, wet, dirty and dangerous. A 70kg roof support leg fell on my workmate Phil. I was the youngest, but found myself taking charge and I got Phil out to safety (minus a finger), without being at all fazed, a scenario I related during my successful interview with South Yorkshire Police.

Training school followed, which got off to a poor start when the drill sergeant asked me my name.

"Richard, sergeant."

The veins on the sergeant's forehead swelled and his face turned blood red as he screamed: "YOUR NAME IS YOUR RANK AND SURNAME!! FIRST NAMES ARE FOR SISSY'S.

ARE YOU A SISSY? RICHARD IS IT? RICHARD? WELL, YOU LOOK LIKE A DICK TO ME!"

As a result, I have been known professionally as Dick for the past 39 years but my family have always only known me as Rich or Richard.

Apart from that blip, I made it through without too many more problems and now here I was, an all-powerful police officer. I'd never forgotten the day this lad, who'd been quite a bit older and bigger than me, along with three of his mates, had attacked me, broken my nose, blackened both my eyes and cracked some ribs.

I removed him from the house and arrested him for public order offences. He pleaded guilty at court and he never knew that his arresting officer was the little auburn-haired boy he'd beaten up ten years previously.

My Christmas dinner may have been cold that day but it tasted damn good to me.

While working as a detective constable in Rotherham, I investigated a woman who'd stolen money from a gas meter. She quickly confessed, citing hard times and depression as excuses. She was a rough diamond and I used to see her in various pubs around Rotherham. I'd say 'Hi,' now and again. We met again professionally after she found herself on the receiving end of criminality, having been burgled. Once I'd taken her statement, she pointed to some tarot cards on the table and asked if I wanted a reading.

"Go on then, for a laugh," I said, as I didn't – and still don't – believe in anything like this.

She started with a few generic things about me that anyone could guess before mentioning I'd been hospitalised recently, which was true. She then told me that my marriage would dissolve in my forties and that I would remarry.

And then she pulled out the death card. Several times.

She looked concerned.

"Am I going to die?" I asked.

"No," she said, "But, oh dear, this just doesn't make any sense. This is the beginning of your midlife; you're surrounded by death, but it's not you. Death just keeps on repeating and repeating. You're steeped in it. I can't explain it."

She then said that death disappeared out of my life in my mid-50s, and was replaced by many children.

"I've never seen anything like this," she said, shaking her head, looking deeply troubled, as I left. "The death just disappears, as quickly as it comes."

I quickly forgot about this, as my thoughts were all full of family and career. I was interviewed for the CID department in a pub – a classic CID move in those days – was accepted in at 23-years-old and, a month after CID training was complete, I was able to take my inspector's exam. The only catch was that Jen was heavily pregnant with our second child and my exam was scheduled for the expected birthdate – April 20. We hoped that Jen would give birth before or after this date but by sheer luck the exam venue happened to be next door to the hospital, so if the worst came to the worst then, I imagined, I could flit between the two.

Of course Jen went into labour in the small hours of April 20, so I took her to hospital then left for my exam dizzy with excitement. I rushed through everything, finishing as fast as I could and then sprinted back to the hospital and made it in time for the birth (Jen said she hung on for me). It was the most marvellous, magical and incredible experience of my life. And I passed my inspector's exam.

In 1988 I was 31-years-old and becoming a seasoned cop, although I was still learning and jobs could still catch me out. I was called to an abattoir on the outskirts of Sheffield where there had been a series of thefts. The owner asked if I wanted to have a look around. I said that I would, and explained about Grandad and his pigs, that I was a seasoned observer of animal slaughter. We stepped into the killing floor and I watched as sheep, pigs, cows and bullocks were herded into a room, alive, noisy and scared until they were all at once silenced by electrocution. Their throats were then slit en-masse before being hung on a mechanical carousel of hooks that whisked them off, still spraying blood, through 10ft-high plastic curtains. The speed and volume was devastating. I left the abattoir utterly distressed. This was no way to slaughter animals.

In 1990 I was invited to join the serious crime squad as a Detective Sergeant. We were a major incident support team and when not called upon we concentrated on target criminals within South Yorkshire. In 1992 we were transformed into a surveillance unit, which meant specialist training – including the advanced driver's course. Sitting about for hours in cars and hiding in hedge bottoms did not really do it for me. It was rare to actually catch a criminal in the act during surveillance (although when it did happen, it was a massive adrenaline surge and very fulfilling). So, although surveillance had its moments, they were too few and far between for me – a cop who loved the 'Life on Mars' lifestyle. I was ready to try and advance to Inspector, so presented myself before a promotion board in May 1993. I succeeded but had to wait until the appropriate appointment came up. In August 1993, I was in the middle of a murder investigation, hiding in a hedge at the bottom of a quarry, when the Chief Constable called me in for a talk. I couldn't think why, and said so.

"You stupid idiot," my boss told me. "It's about getting promoted, straight from DS to DI and staying in CID."

Wow, this was amazing news. Aged only 34, I'd be the youngest DI in South Yorkshire Police. But the Chief soon wiped the grin from my face. The promotion was a sweetener for a job no one else wanted. I had to join the understaffed Fraud Squad, 8am to 4pm, Monday to Friday, no overtime and not an ounce of interest for me. Grey men in grey suits with about 700 years' service. This was as about as far away from what I'd wanted to do as was possible.

"Do this a couple of years and then you can move on," the Chief told me, "I'm sure there will be a good posting waiting for you at Division."

So, on 3 August 1993, complete with pinstriped suit, I took up post as Detective Inspector, Fraud Squad. The team consisted of a Detective Chief Inspector, myself, twenty Detective Constables and some Police (Civilian) Staff.

Two days in and I got my welcome meeting with the Detective Chief Superintendent. I told him that he was speaking to a man who didn't even get his maths O-Level, hoping that he would see that I probably was not the best man for the job after all.

"Don't worry about that Dick," he said, dashing my hopes, "You'll do just fine. Oh, and by the way, when we get the next Hillsborough, Fraud Squad are responsible for deceased victims and temporary mortuaries."

This sentence, tagged on at the end of our meeting, hit me with the physical force of a hammer blow. I'd been at Hillsborough on the day of the disaster.

April 15, 1989. Clear blue skies, the sense of summer approaching and the prospect of an FA Cup semi-final match between top Championship rivals Liverpool and Nottingham Forest, played on the neutral ground of Sheffield Wednesday's Hillsborough Stadium.

Thirteen years a cop, I was a plain-clothed CID sergeant but had squeezed back into an ill-fitting uniform after volunteering for twelve hours of overtime, policing the grounds from 8am to 8pm, during which I would have a chance to see some footballing legends in action up close.

Instead, I witnessed a tragedy that left 96 dead and 766 injured, the result of crushing in the overcrowded stadium.

At the time of writing, the second inquest into the disaster is underway and so it would not be appropriate for me to relate my experiences at this time. Once the inquest and subsequent possible criminal investigation is complete, a chapter that covers my experiences at Hillsborough on that day will be made available as a free download from amazon.co.uk and from my agent's website, andrewlownie.co.uk.

For now, suffice it to say, I visited Anfield (which had been declared a shrine) shortly after the disaster. I went with a friend, DC Tony Cawkwell, one of the best thief takers I've ever worked with. Dressed in sweatshirts and jeans and we queued at the Bill Shankly Gates. I struggled desperately to hold it together as the countless tributes left at the Spion Kop end came into view. The victims became truly real to me then. They had mostly been young with full lives ahead of them. Their friends and families had been left with unimaginable grief.

I know that everything I felt – and still do – cannot compare with the torment of the families of the people that died that day; people that should have survived – would have survived if they'd been treated sooner.

Cops are responders. We come running after an incident has happened. It's extremely rare for cops to witness incidents, let alone witness loss of life and to see a major disaster take place right before your eyes, while you, in police uniform stand helplessly by unable to satisfy the basic principal of policing – to protect.

I'd seen people die right in front of me and I'd been unable to help them. I will feel the guilt for the rest of my life. It is real, permanent, devastating. Flashbacks strike whenever life's not going so well. I know I'm not the only one.

Lord Justice Taylor's report into Hillsborough was published just before I joined the Fraud Squad. It was scathing about South Yorkshire Police, confirming what many already felt: we'd not only failed to do our job, we weren't fit for purpose. The report led to the realisation within the Police Service that new attitudes towards dealing with major disasters were needed.

At the time, the Taylor report – added to my already strong personal feelings – made me want to disassociate myself with ever being at Hillsborough. But my DCS's comment about the mortuaries reawakened memories and emotions. I thought I had locked away but they were there, floating just below my consciousness, and I had simply become good at pushing them down when they threatened to resurface. Now they came to the fore and I was overcome with guilt – and realised that there was no getting rid of these memories or feelings.

I started to think that perhaps I could use my experience at Hillsborough, to some good purpose. I had many 'fight or flight' moments during those initial weeks as I tried to think of strategies. In the panicky flight moments, thoughts snuck in about leaving it, or sorting out minimal, periphery-type stuff which would satisfy the bosses that I was doing something about it, and then move on after two years as the Chief had advised. Besides, Fraud and temporary mortuaries hardly seemed to go hand-in-glove.

But I continued to examine and think about the subject; I just couldn't ignore it; something in me had been kindled. As a police force and as a country, we were lacking in terms of our response to major disasters. This had to be changed and, for whatever reason, I was going to be a part of that change. I began to ask myself seemingly impossible questions, such as: 'What can *we* do to help grieving families to come to terms with their loss?'

By this time in my police service, I was a confident police officer. I knew what I could and couldn't do. Like all police officers, I'd acquired certain mechanical skills necessary to survive the job. I would like to think that I learned how to be practical rather than harsh, although police officers in general have to take a somewhat hardened approach, else we wouldn't cope with all the horrible things we have to deal with.

I'd worked on thirty murders and countless sudden deaths and I knew I was not good at delivering bad news, neither was I emotionally intelligent when it came to dealing with the bereaved. Dead bodies, on the other hand, I could handle. I thought perhaps if I concentrated on this aspect of my brief and the positive impact that dealing with the dead could have upon relatives, if, for example, they could at least know that the body of their loved one was being treated with dignity and respect, then that may at least give them some comfort. After all, I thought, as professionals, we owe it to families to do our very best for them at the worst time in their lives.

The only problem was I didn't know where to start.

FOUR

GETTING STARTED

I was standing in front of twenty grey-suited, office-bound and mostly overweight members of Fraud Squad detectives who were looking at me open-mouthed in shock and disbelief. I'd just explained that, should a major disaster talk place in South Yorkshire then we were responsible for dead bodies and temporary mortuaries.

An explosion of expletives followed, coming thick and fast in between phrases such as "You've got to be joking," and "This is some kind of wind-up right?"

"What have we done to deserve this being dumped upon us?" one ashen-faced detective demanded.

I rolled out my strategic answer, hoping they wouldn't smell the bull.

"Our bosses believe that fraud investigators are the best in the Force because of their methodology and attention to detail."

The real reason was that no one else wanted the job and it was thought that the Grey Squad could be plucked out of their day job at any time and parachuted back in without being missed because what they did took so bloody long.

I agreed with them, however. I knew from Hillsborough what happened when officers were exposed to something of that magnitude with no or very little training, without any preparation. Also, I already knew there were some officers in this team that I felt would never be able to deal effectively with dead and mutilated bodies. With this in mind, one of my first representations to the powers that be was that this kind of work should only be carried out by officers who volunteered for the role. I argued that volunteer officers could be brought in from many different departments and Divisions and, as such, no one department or unit would suffer from the delay in their day-to-day crime-fighting jobs caused by the sudden removal of all of their officers.

Even this didn't solve the problem of course. Volunteering is one thing. Taking part in an actual deployment is something else. Some people might suddenly realise that they were mistaken and weren't able to cope with the recovery and identification of the deceased when we needed them most. The only way to 'test' these volunteers was to put them through some kind of training that involved role-play.

The powers that be agreed with both my points and so I set about researching the science of disaster. The nearest connection to this new world that I could find was South Yorkshire's Casualty Bureau, run by John Griffiths, a retired sergeant who had spent many years training police officers in a variety of roles. The Casualty Bureau's computer system keeps a constantly updated record of those reported missing and potentially involved and is where relatives are asked to call in the event of a major disaster. John was immediately intrigued by the prospect of designing a completely new training package which looked at the whole process; from initial reports of missing people, through recovery, identification and uniting the bereaved with their deceased loved-one. He sought the advice of Graham Owen, an Inspector from Doncaster who would eventually become the Force Contingency Planning Officer, and we began to put together a training package aimed at preparing officers to locate and recover bodies and body parts, to assist the pathologist in the mortuary to establish identification and, on behalf of HM Coroner, to return the deceased to their family at the earliest opportunity. Systems for this procedure had been in place at Coroner's Offices for many years but when multiple deaths occur from a disaster scenario, it's a totally different ball game. Confusion and overload are almost instantaneous and this had never been addressed.

Our aim was to provide our volunteers with a five-day course. We were the only provincial force in the country doing this at the time and so we had to create the model from nothing. The Metropolitan Police had a body recovery team stationed at Heathrow; there was a myth at the time that aircraft disasters were the ones most likely to occur and that they would do so at the airport for added convenience. On average, five hundred people per year die in aviation incidents across the world, which has been the same since 1945, despite the huge increase in aviation traffic. So, flying remains the safest mode of transport.

It was rare for the Met to share any of its training with provincial Forces (in fact, it was almost unheard of), but the Inspector from the Heathrow team, Gerry Jackson, agreed to assist us. He had, among other mass fatality incidents, been involved with body recovery at Lockerbie, so we learned all we could from him. The Lockerbie disaster took place on December 21 1988, when the Pan Am jet *Maid of the Seas* had been blown up by Libyan terrorists over a small Scottish town resulting in 270 fatalities (I had flown on that very jet on a holiday to Florida in August the same year).

The 1980s were known as the 'decade of disaster': the Bradford City Stadium Fire (May '85), the Manchester Airport Disaster (Aug '85), the Sumburgh Chinook Crash (Nov '86), the sinking of the Herald of Free Enterprise (Mar '87), the Kings Cross Fire (Nov '87), the Piper Alpha oil rig fire (Jul '88), the Lockerbie Air Disaster (Dec '88), the Kegworth Air Disaster (Jan '89), Hillsborough (April '89) and the sinking of the Marchioness (Aug '89).

We invited officers who had been involved in some of these incidents to speak on the course and tell us about their experiences; how they responded, how they completed identifications and how they felt. It wasn't just about the process; we also needed to know how they had been affected emotionally at the time and afterwards.

No one was more effective at conveying this than Mark Rand, an ex- Chief Superintendent with West Yorkshire Police, who came to speak about the Bradford Stadium Fire of May 11 1985, the worst fire disaster in the history of English football in which 56 people died and 265 were injured. I've since seen Mark's presentation on over twenty occasions and it never fails to move me.

Finally, an insight into the operational side in terms of what happens in the first few hours at a mass fatality incident scene, the chaos and mayhem that ensues, was provided by Paul Gibson, a Chief Superintendent from Leicestershire who was involved in recovery operations after the Kegworth air crash of January 8, 1989 when British Midland Flight 92 crashed on an embankment of the M1, killing 47 of the 126 people on board. 74 people, including seven members of the flight crew, suffered serious injury. All of these elements made for a decent training package in terms of learning from those who had 'been there'

As our knowledge grew, I became more and more obsessed with this aspect of my work, over and above my day job; it had become a passion.

We met with occupational health specialists who educated us in post-incident welfare, especially in relation to hazardous materials and environments and, after this we decided to use a 'live' exercise scenario to experiment with the practical recovery of victims, through a body holding area to the mortuary where identification would take place. The first such exercise took place in 1994 and didn't exactly go to plan. The live volunteers we used as bodies at the 'scene' proved to be surprisingly different to work with as opposed to a dead one, especially when accidents took place. In one case a stretcher split and our 'body' cracked her head on the ground, leaving her in need of medical attention. We then replaced the live volunteers with mannequins, except for the identification process, which takes place in the mortuary, as it was more effective to work with a live human who played dead for their undressing and the recording of their personal details and property. It may seem bizarre, but it was the nearest we could get to training for the real thing.

We also needed to expose our volunteers to dead bodies. In this line of work it's crucial to know how a cadaver feels and how it smells, so one is not overwhelmed in a real situation. It's also a good way of weeding out anyone who might not be able to hack it. The Coroner of South Yorkshire (West), Christopher Dorries, had only recently taken up his post but he welcomed us into his mortuary and we set to work – with the caveat that trainees would not be exposed to criminal cases (due to the integrity of evidence), or cases involving children.[1]

The first courses were held during summer. Oddly, fewer people seem to die in the summer months and we struggled to find enough bodies for our volunteers to work with. When we did, our students flaked out all the time. This didn't necessarily mean they weren't suitable; a large part of it is to do with one's fitness on the day, and how much adrenaline happens to be pumping through your system. No one is immune.

---

1 Despite never having presided over a mass fatality incident as a Coroner himself, Christopher Dorries (who has been the Coroner for South Yorkshire (West) since 1991) has remained incredibly supportive in developing DVI and multi agency awareness since day one. He has helped enormously in terms of the UK's preparedness for mass fatality incidents and was awarded an OBE in 2006 for his work on emergency planning.

My daughter had been unwell during the second course and had had ended up in hospital. I spent all night with her, didn't sleep at all and went straight to the mortuary. As the process started, I went out like a light. Another important lesson. I needed to be mindful on the day, of where the officers were in terms of their 'fitness' to proceed; in case they were ill or hadn't had a chance to get some rest, for example.

The other thing during these courses was for me to learn to spot the signs that someone was 'about to go'. I was normally assisted by John and Graham and before the examinations began I put myself in England Cricket Captain mode: I would set my field, strategically placing my assistants in positions where each of us could spot any potential fainter and catch them before they dropped. I used to joke to the pathologist that I had set two slips and a gully and he could now proceed.

We would usually spot the vulnerable ones and catch them before they hit the floor but there was one incident when a cop fainted, going down with quite some force and the pathologist simply said dryly: "Pick him up and put him on the other table and I'll get to him in a minute."

By May 1995, I had run three courses, trained 55 officers and had been asked to deliver the course regionally. It seemed to be a success but it was impossible to judge until I had some practical experience. And when something did happen, the Force would look to me to act, and the pressure would be on (especially as whatever happened would be the first disaster since Hillsborough). An odd collection of thoughts gathered in my mind, and I hovered between terror at the thought of what might happen, the desire for experience, the fear of responsibility, the fear of failure and the knowledge that my job depended upon terrible events in which many people would die.

FIVE

NEVER SEEN IT SO BAD

Wednesday May 24, 1995. A hot, hazy day; muggy and close. Storms rolled in late in the afternoon. Driving rain – large, bouncing drops driven from heavy black clouds that cracked with thunder.

I was in my kitchen, tea on, radio in the background, watching in awe as the storm's tempo grew and bolts of lightning lit the dark hills for miles around.

"We're receiving reports that a light aircraft has crashed in West Yorkshire...Carrying nine passengers and three crew...crashed on Dunkeswick Moor...pieces of the plane were strewn..."

Putting on the TV, I switched to the early evening news, which was leading with the crash. A Bandeirante aircraft, a twin-turboprop light passenger aircraft carrying nine passengers and three crew had gone into a nose dive and broken up in mid-air before crashing in a barley field next to the A61 on Dunkeswick Moor. It had crashed after taking off just a few minutes earlier at 5.47pm in stormy weather from Leeds-Bradford Airport.

I watched as a spokesman from Knight Air, the operator, gave a media briefing, exuding the 'three Ps'; pity, praise and promise. Police Supervisory Officers and other public officials receive training in how to talk to the media, and in techniques that send a positive message in the face of adversity, particularly when speaking about an incident that involves death. After expressing sympathy and regret, one is supposed to try to give some comfort to those affected (usually through praise for the efforts of all the emergency services and other responders), then promise to do all in their power to find out the cause and bring the perpetrator (if applicable), or any culpable person or organisation to justice. Despite the man's professionalism, he couldn't conceal his emotions.

My first thought, "My God that's twelve families whose lives have changed forever," was quickly followed by the realisation that identification of the twelve deceased would be difficult; body parts would need precise identification and matching for the families.

I grabbed the phone and rang John. "Do you think we should offer our assistance?"

The plane had crashed in an area that was on our neighbour's – North Yorkshire's – patch, and with no officers trained in disaster response they might appreciate the offer. Both John and Graham agreed, so we let it be known we were available if needed. The Assistant Chief Constable of Operations in South Yorkshire Police approached North Yorkshire and they decided to allow us to attend in the capacity of observers and advisers, so that North Yorks would be able to tap into our theoretical experience.

The Lead Pathologist dealing with the fatalities from this disaster was John Clark, who at that time covered the whole of Yorkshire. He had worked with us during our training and he was totally on board with the concept and practices that we were trying to establish. Our initial remit – apart from observing and advising – was to be John's 'loaders and shifters'; we were to pick up a van the following day and stock it with mortuary equipment to take up to the temporary mortuary site.

When the late evening news came on, it sunk in. I was actually being deployed. Before long I was having huge adrenalin surges, almost to the point of palpitations. It wasn't panic; I was a cop with almost twenty years' service and I had learned to manage the 'arousal curve' way back; professionalism always kicks in. It was more to do with the unknown: Would I cope? Would I take to it as easily as I always thought I would? Would I remain absolutely professional? Would I end up as a leader or as a bystander? And what if I got something wrong?

What a big fall that would be. If I did end up being heavily involved, this was going to be the biggest test of my life. Yet I felt excited. This was a chance to *do* something positive rather than to just talk about it.

I knew the procedures inside-out, but the human aspect played on my mind. Although I told myself that I just needed to remember the process and to remain professional, I made the mistake of continuing to watch the evening news, which had started give details and show photographs of the deceased. I didn't want to take in their details. I didn't want to 'create' the person in my head. I didn't want it personalised before I had even been deployed. Yet I held the same morbid fascinations as many other people. Who were they? How had they died (in an explosion or in the impact)? What did the scene look like?

I watched.

Of the twelve people, six were from West Yorkshire and six were from Scotland. Nine were male; three were female. New 'what ifs' kept arriving in my mind unprompted, chief among them being: Were any of them children? Not that anyone is, but I'd never been good with child deaths, which seem to occur all-too frequently, from cot deaths to road traffic accidents. And then there are the accidental deaths that occur during play, where children, being naturally curious adventurous, sometimes don't realize the danger they're in. I was once called to a house in Rotherham where a boy had hanged himself from the bannister by his scarf while pretending to be Tarzan. Like most people, I find it deeply disturbing how life can be so unjustly robbed from the very young. The news item suggested there weren't any children involved in the air crash but I wanted to be totally certain about this before the process started, so that I wouldn't be thrown by it.

Despite my many concerns and worries about the unknowns I was surprised to awaken on Thursday morning feeling refreshed. I met John and Graham at 7am. Along with Graham, I'd dressed in accordance with our given remit of 'removals' men (blue jeans and denim shirt), but John arrived in his best suit, collar and tie. He liked to be smart, no matter the circumstances.

We collected a Transit Freight Rover Van from one of South Yorkshire Polices' transport depots and drove to the Medico Legal Centre where we loaded up a dozen mortuary tables and other general mortuary equipment. As the only Police driver amongst the three of us with a permit for this class of vehicle, I drove the van up to the RAF base at Linton-on-Ouse. This large and busy airbase, where RAF jet pilots are trained, had been designated as the temporary mortuary site, twenty miles from the scene.

We grew quieter the nearer we got. I remember nothing about the journey except that the same thoughts kept cycling through my head: would I be able to hack it? What if I failed? This wasn't an option of course, but it pressed heavily upon me. I'm the kind of person who, as apprehension grows, the quieter I become.

At this time, security was tight due to threats from Irish terrorism and we drew up at the military gates at 11am to be welcomed by four soldiers armed with machine guns. They directed us to the sports hall, where there was no access control, so we simply wandered in.

That was the first shock, a strange one too. I expected to walk in and see what I had seen at the Medico Centre Mortuary: tiled walls, flooring, drainage and lighting. What we actually walked into was what it said on the tin; a sports hall with clearly-marked courts for badminton and basketball.

It was filled with people, some in uniform; some in civvies. I was a bit baffled as to who the heck they all were. Some guys in suits were just in front of us and erecting six-foot tripods, mounting them with arc lights and to my right cricket nets were being pulled back to the wall.

Graham's counterpart, the Force Contingency Planning Officer from North Yorkshire, 'Tad', came over to greet us. He was very welcoming and, still anxious about what we were about to deal with I blurted out: "Are any children involved? Just like to know in advance."

"No Dick, no children."

"Thanks," I breathed a sigh of relief. "Glad to hear that at least."

We set about unloading the van as partitions went up, dividing about a third of the sports hall into a mortuary. They took the mortuary tables we had delivered and placed them widthways across the hall, which kind of went against my expectations, as I envisaged they'd be set up like swimming lanes, with tables laid out longways.

The tables themselves were 6ft 6" long by 2ft 9" wide, made of stainless steel. They had big tubular-shaped handles as part of the frame, enabling them to double up as metal stretchers. They had a slight gradient with a plughole at the lowest end for drainage. The tables didn't come with legs but some clever person had designed stands for them, which were wooden and looked a bit like a DIY workbench, being triangular in shape. Two of these stands slotted into grooves on the underneath of the tables to make a steady and sturdy mortuary table. In terms of the practicalities of the DVI process this set up was ideal as it was easy to lift the table off the grooves and move the body or body part around on the metal stretcher to the various specialist areas (i.e., from strip-and-search to X-Ray, to odontology, to pathology, etc.) rather than for the specialists to move around to the body or body part. Those tables and stands are probably still as fit for purpose today in this context as they were back then.

My anxiety faded as we joined in with the mortuary set up and we were kept busy throughout the day. I was, however, left somewhat deflated after a senior officer, accompanied by his deputy, eventually came over to speak with us. They were civil enough, but it was clear they wanted us kept at arm's length. They weren't interested in our training and what we'd learned. It seemed obvious to me that we would be kept very much in the background during the DVI process. Instead, they were doting on a member of the national Major Disaster Advisory Team (MDAT) who had come up from Manchester to assist. He had experience 'in the field' from a plane crash at Manchester Airport in 1985, when a holiday jet bound for Corfu caught fire whilst taxiing on the runway, causing the deaths of 54 people. Once I spoke to the MDAT member, it was clear that he was not up-to-date with current thinking, theory and practices and when he said: "I hope they're not relying on me!" I became concerned. I genuinely felt for the bloke, as it was clear that he was a 'one-hit-wonder' and I think he realised that he was out of his depth. His briefing lacked confidence. He kept it too generic, i.e., "you're going to see some sights here and you will remember them forever" and "you will have sleepless nights after this." This was important to an extent psychologically speaking, but I wanted to hear about the actual process that the teams would be going through and how it was going to be managed. There was nothing about how things should be done, nothing about expectations of the staff in their professional capacities and nothing about why the teams were actually there – for the bereaved of the deceased and to do them justice. I was bursting to interrupt and ask questions but I felt it would be unfair to put him on the spot. I also held back a bit because I wasn't totally confident in my own abilities, or how I would cope when faced with the all-too-real scenario of actual bodies and body parts.

Shortly afterwards, I tentatively approached this senior officer and asked him what I had been burning to find out during the briefing – how all of this was actually going to be done. I had taken a PowerPoint presentation and some mortuary notes with me from part of the training course we delivered and asked if he and some of the others wanted to have a look. They did and I shared some of my thoughts and learning with them. They weren't impressed. Perhaps my expectations were too high but if that was the case then it was only a result of my passion and enthusiasm to get the job done right. I just remember thinking that there was a noticeable lack of clarity and a possible lack in knowledge but I had more chance of getting hit by a snowball in the Sahara than getting through to anyone here. Luckily, I was at least proved wrong by Dr. Clark who shared his plans for the actual process and encouraged our involvement, and we did end up adding some of our research to the following day's briefing.

The bodies were to go through strip and search, autopsy, dentistry (odontology), fingerprints and for the two pilots, X-ray, in order to try to establish causation (in case one or both had developed a medical condition that caused the accident) and identification.

Later that Thursday afternoon, military vehicles started to bring the bodies that had been recovered from the scene, onto the site. The body bags were placed in rows to the right of the main doors, behind a low wall that marked out the five-a-side pitch. I had an immense sense of anticipation and curiosity. I went over to where they were being laid. The first thought that struck me was, 'God, what odd shapes'. And then the realisation really hit that the bodies were not likely to be in 'normal' human form. The bags were irregular, with parts sticking up or out at different angles and were in varying sizes.

We were not going to start the process until 8am the next morning and so I was left with sixteen hours of curiosity to contend with. I desperately wanted to take a quick look inside one of the bags. Not for any weird, morbid reason, just so that my eyes and brain would know what to expect, rather than leaving my overactive imagination to run wild through the night.

I was suddenly yanked out of my thoughts by a familiar cockney accent.

"Alright Dick. How are you mate? Have they got you in to do the mortuary?"

It was Gerry Jackson who was helping to bring in one of the bodies. He'd been drafted up from Heathrow to assist with victim recovery at the scene. We caught up with each other's news; it was extremely odd to talk like this, considering what was around us. Gerry and his team had been working in awful conditions, trying to recover bodies and body parts from a field deep in barely while a storm raged around them. As Gerry made to leave, his parting shot was: "Good luck to you pal, you'll certainly be able to cut your teeth on this one. I've never seen anything as bad as this."

If Gerry was saying that after what he'd seen at Lockerbie, then what the hell was in those bags? I waved him off as if nothing was wrong but the hairs on the back of my neck were standing on end and goose bumps pricked my skin. Panicked thoughts raced through my mind again: "Why have you got into this? Why are you here, Dick?"

Suddenly I thought of Grandad's pigs. Surely there was nothing worse than seeing a healthy pig stunned and systematically bled to death. I pulled myself together. The damage had already been done; the bereaved were already grieving, nothing could be done to bring their loved ones back. But it was in our gift to treat them with the respect and dignity they deserved and to give them closure. Just focus on the job in hand. By the end of the process, we had to be confident that each body and body part had been correctly identified as belonging to an individual deceased victim, so that relatives and friends would be assured that the body or body parts returned to them belonged to their loved one.

My thoughts were broken again, this time by chatter around the need to refrigerate the bodies. It had been a fine, pleasant day, around twenty degrees and it was warm in the sports hall. As plans were being made to bring in refrigerated units for body storage, I left for home. It was around 4pm.

That evening my confidence pinged between having little to lots in seconds and as I went to bed, expecting a restlessness night, for the first time in years I felt well out of my professional comfort zone.

SIX

THE UNZIPPING

First thing the next morning, I joined Dr. Clark and his team (there were three teams altogether), along with five Police Officers, including a photographer, with clipboards and forms ready. We gathered around the mortuary station, all dressed in white wellies and white Tyvek suits (like the ones you've probably seen on TV), see-through rubber gloves and facemasks. Facemasks had been recommended but they weren't compulsory and all of us soon ended up with the masks perched on the tops of our heads. We looked like conference of Popes.

The first body, still in the opaque white bag, was stretchered in and rested on the trestles. We were expecting it to be one of the two pilots. One was extremely experienced, in his fifties; the other in his twenties, had been at the beginning of his career.

For incidents such as Dunkeswick, straightforward visual identification is unreliable, mainly due to the fact that bodies are often not in an identifiable state. Asking relatives and loved ones to view victims to confirm identification is simply not acceptable. Sudden bereavement is near impossible to come to terms with in the immediate aftermath, and there have been cases of non-recognition as the bereaved so desperately want it to not be their loved one who has died. For these reasons, the DVI process becomes even more important. In essence, for each and every body and body part of a victim involved in a mass fatality disaster, it is the role of the police to satisfy the Coroner, via matching ante-mortem (information from friends, work colleagues and families, for example) and post-mortem data, as to why they believe body or body part number 'x' belongs to person 'y'. The Police do not have the power to confirm identity; only the Coroner can do this based on the evidence presented.

John Clark had confidently delivered that morning's briefing, leaving no doubt as to who would be leading this – him. Although DNA testing existed in 1995, it was unreliable and incredibly expensive. So the accepted scientific criteria were odontology (dentistry) and fingerprints, with confirmation of identity via personal effects. Also, 'mechanical fit' would be used for the many body parts that would arrive in their own separate body bags. If the parts could be 'pieced together' precisely enough to prove that they belonged to the same person, then this could also be submitted as supporting evidence.

As well as looking for clues as to the identity of each victim, we had to determine as far as possible, whether anything about their bodies could tell us how the plane had crashed. As the investigation into the cause was proceeding with great speed, we needed to examine the pilots first to establish whether something like a heart attack or seizure could have caused the crash, or if either pilot had been drinking or taking drugs, for example.

The paperwork was checked. The victim recovery forms completed at the scene had remained with the body. They detailed the location that the body had been recovered from (close to the cockpit) and the fact that officers at the scene had been able to spot the pilot's insignia on his uniform. It seemed to me as though all details had been precisely and professionally recorded.

That done, it was almost time to open the bag. A flash of apprehension passed through me as I recalled Gerry's comments about the bodies. I looked down at the white bag and thought, "You know what mate? This is the easy bit." This might sound awful, even disrespectful to some, but I had conditioned myself to not see whatever was in the bag as someone. What was there was merely a vehicle, a shell that had taken the person through life.

I turned my gaze from the bag to look at the other people around the table and saw fear. Pure fear on every one of the police officers' faces. I knew then that I was right to only ever use officers who had volunteered to do this kind of work – and had been trained. These poor buggers were simply picked because they were on duty that day. Despite their professionalism and willingness to do what was asked, they just weren't prepared.

What made things much worse for them was that they had never seen the impossibly complex Interpol forms before. They didn't know where to start. These forms are the internationally recognized standard paperwork on which data is recorded about a deceased individual and are supposed to assist in identifying them. I say 'supposed' because they dictated to the writer rather than assisting the process as a tool for gathering evidence. They were excessively detailed and overly complex. Details such as the length of a foot ante-mortem compared with post-mortem as an identifying feature are next to useless in reality, as there is so much room for error. Any Coroner worth their salt would never accept such 'evidence' to assist with identity so this, together with many other parts of the Interpol forms was pointless. They slowed the process and were simply not user friendly. But filling them out was a legal requirement, so I had studied them and knew how they worked, and would be able to assist with this.

It was also quite possible that some of these officers hadn't even seen a dead body before, never mind a disrupted one. I found it hard to believe we were facing this situation (at least in part because in South Yorkshire we were advanced in training DVI volunteers).

If I thought I was struggling how the hell were they feeling? It had gone quiet and I could see each officer was lost in their own versions of what I'd been thinking about, except I at least had a bit of grounding in this line of work. I cleared my throat and started talking. A bit of conversation might keep their minds occupied, I thought, and help to suppress any fits of fainting.

I chatted about how I saw the body as a vehicle and then started to talk about the process, what they were going to be doing and more importantly why. "I'm trained to do this and I'm not exactly finding it easy myself; it's my first time, too."

I wanted them to understand that what they were thinking and feeling was entirely normal in what was a totally abnormal situation. I became acutely conscious of the other officers at the two other stations and wondered how John and Graham were getting on.

Dr. Clark took hold of the bag's zip and pulled. I think that initial sound and its movement downwards was pretty harrowing for everyone, including the pathologist, as even they don't see things like this often.

The body was severely disrupted and wasn't whole; it was hard to see the "person" it had once been. I shouldn't have been surprised. After all, a large piece of metal had fallen out of the sky at around 200mph. That guy wouldn't have known much about it.

There was very little blood. I breathed in. I thought the smell would be unpleasant, like the smell of death I had experienced so many times previously. But it wasn't anything like that. The smell was earthy and metallic. It's odd, having one's sensory expectations confounded; the lack of blood and the fact there was no particular smell, I think helped the others relax a little. The reality was less horrific than imagined. I was confident that if the cops could cope with this they could cope with the next couple of days and would get through it ok.

I noticed the pilot insignia, four stripes. And so the process began. Although two police officers were designated to strip the body to remove and log all clothing and personal effects, John Clark and his Pathology technician decided that they would actually lead on this, possibly recognising that the cops were a little out of their depth. They carefully handed each item that they removed to the two police officers who examined them, and wrote down a detailed description for logging, looking for any clues that might help with identification, whilst another officer did their best to navigate the Interpol forms in time to record all of the details. Each item of clothing and each piece of property found on the body was removed, examined and fully described before being photographed and placed in separate exhibit bags. Once stripped of all clothing and personal effects, the body itself was examined for any distinguishing marks, scars, tattoos, abnormalities, etc. Any found were recorded on the forms. Every single piece of information regarding what was in that white opaque bag had to be captured with precise accuracy together with everything that John Clark mentioned in relation to the condition of the body throughout the autopsy.

This part of the process took about one hour, with a great deal of time taken up by the complex Interpol forms. The officers were learning, in a very harsh and extreme way, but they were at least learning.

Once the first part of the process had been completed, the body was moved from the strip-and-search and autopsy station to odontology. Odontology is a scientific means of identification, which is very precise and inexpensive. Most people have dental treatment during their life and the more treatment they have, the more unique their dental charts will be. Even fillings are done differently and so can be distinctive on their own. The odontologists within the mortuary carefully log evidence of any dental treatment that they can find from the deceased victim so, provided that the ante-mortem dental records are kept up to date these can be matched and identification confirmed, usually very quickly and with 100% accuracy, making Odontology matching extremely reliable.

When the odontologist had completed their examinations, the first body was moved to the fingerprint station. I noticed that one of the fingerprint officers wasn't much more than twenty years old (I later found out that she'd only just completed her training). She didn't look as though she was going to cope and I considered stepping in, but it occurred to me this would make things worse for her. To do so would professionally embarrass her; perhaps she would have insisted that she was fine, and on staying (when she was not, especially after I'd brought this to everyone's attention), but then would have double the pressure as more eyes would be upon her. Nevertheless, she had to fingerprint all twelve victims and I could see, as time went on, that the psychological pressure was too much. She got through it but not, I fear, unscathed.

The first body then went through to x-ray, still with every finding being recorded. The police officers needed the experience in all aspects and so took turns to scribe the details for each part of the process until eventually, we were done.

I hadn't realized quite how important stamina was. After an hour spent on the initial examination, undressing, autopsy and the relevant form filling, odontology, fingerprints and X-Ray had each taken about thirty minutes to complete. That's two-and-a-half hours of standing, with nowhere for anyone to take a seat if they felt they needed a rest. But after that first body, I was full of adrenalin, as well as relief that we'd managed to successfully complete the process. I'd coped and was ready to continue. As I kept telling myself, it wasn't rocket science; it was all about coping with the unpleasant facts of sudden and violent death while completing each step of the identification process in a professional manner.

After a few more hours, I noticed John had approached. He beckoned me to one side. "Are you alright Dick?" he asked quietly. I have to admit I didn't take the question in the spirit in which it was asked. John and Graham had both been as apprehensive as I had been but as far as I could tell they looked and sounded as professional as anyone else. I took John's kind concern for my welfare as a sign that he thought I was displaying some physical weakness. I snapped back at him in typical police style: "I'm fine. Why, don't I look like I'm ok?"

While we were working hard at Linton to collect all of the post-mortem evidence, others were working tirelessly to collect ante-mortem evidence, without which, identification cannot happen. Police Family Liaison Officers (FLOs) were gathering dental records of those listed on the flight manifest. They were also visiting the home addresses of the deceased victims and, in extremely difficult circumstances, were trying to lift latent fingerprints from surfaces and items used by the deceased. Most people do not have an official fingerprint record unless they have been a suspect in a crime or convicted of crime so in terms of evidence for the Coroner in these circumstances, latent prints are crucial. There are of course, moral issues when considering the use of official fingerprints such as convictions records, as details are likely to be made public in court. My thoughts are that fingerprints obtained in this way should be used as intelligence-only with lifted latent fingerprints being used for formal identification. The FLOs were also talking with grieving relatives and friends to obtain personal details about clothing worn that day; any marks, scars, tattoos the victims had and any personal items they may have been carrying. All of these elements formed the ante-mortem data – the things that are known about the deceased pre death – and all details, just as with those obtained in the mortuary, were meticulously logged.

It is worth stressing the fact the collection of ante-mortem and post-mortem data happens simultaneously, so those working within the mortuary do not usually see what has been harvested on the ante-mortem side and vice-versa, which means that neither can influence the other and each remains impartial and objective. Also of note is that during mass fatality incidents where large numbers are involved the police will open the Casualty Bureau where again, much ante-mortem information is gathered about a person who is subsequently recorded as being missing and thought to be involved. Dunkeswick didn't require a Casualty Bureau as, thanks to the flight manifest, we knew who was on board the plane and we were dealing with twelve people as opposed to dozens. This was what we termed a Completely Closed Incident, where the numbers and names of deceased are known at the outset. A Completely Open Incident takes place when the authorities have no immediate idea of the number and/or identities of the deceased, for example the 7/7 bombings in London and the 9/11 attacks in New York. The third type of incident is a hybrid of these two, such as when a plane crashes into a populated area (such as the bombing of Pan Am flight 103 when the plane crashed into the village of Lockerbie).

For mass fatality planning, the above classifications can be further sub-divided according to a huge number of variables, such as fragmentation, body completeness, what is visually identifiable, accessibility to the site of the disaster, whether there are any contaminants that could be harmful to the recovery teams or people living nearby, and so on. All have to be taken into account when formulating a Disaster Victim Identification Plan, according to the specifics of a particular incident.

Back in the mortuary for Dunkeswick, I became increasingly uncomfortable with one aspect of the post mortem procedures. Some body parts, large and small, had been bagged separately from the bodies at the site as they had either landed some distance away, or defied a straightforward match. It was decided to keep these parts in the middle of the mortuary space and they were checked, as each examination was completed, for mechanical fit. These parts were left uncovered, awaiting the arrival of the other part(s) that belonged to the same victim.

This seemed wrong to me. Having to constantly look at and circumnavigate these open body bags was disturbing for many people working in the mortuary; people who weren't expected to deal with the bodies. My inexperience within a mortuary environment prevented me from challenging the pathologist who made this decision, but it caused me much anxiety at the time and I decided I would try and find a solution for this. The experience left me in no doubt that the bodies should have been covered and placed back in the refrigerated storage unit, rather than being left out. I am an absolute stalwart that dignity must prevail at all times.

After the pilot's body had been processed, I slipped into automatic mode as we processed the next body, and the next. The pace was rapid but steady and lots of questions were being asked about the process; I was taking in everything I could. By the early afternoon I was pleased with how I was coping and how much I was learning.

The next bag was laid on the table in front of us. Once we all declared ourselves ready, Dr. Clark unzipped it. And I froze. The victim was a young woman in her early twenties. She was the only victim whose face was intact. Unmarked, in fact. My mum's often-repeated remark, that the eyes are the gateway to their soul, leapt into my mind. This woman's eyes were wide open. And I swear, at that moment, I felt I could see to her soul. It took my breath away. Her whole life had been in front of her. And now she was here, with us, eight men in white suits all looking down upon her, trying their best to cope with the extremely difficult task she and her fellow victims presented us.

I realised then that deceased victims who were intact were going to cause me more problems psychologically than those who were disrupted – the opposite of what I'd imagined at the start of this job.

We finished at 6pm on the Friday with a start time of 8am planned for the Saturday. There was no debrief, no diffusing. Twenty minutes after we'd downed tools, John and I were back in my red Mazda and driving out of the base on our way home. I arrived at a T-junction to join the main road when I drove straight out in front of a car that was going 60mph. There was no time to do anything except shut my eyes and grip the wheel. The impact didn't come. Somehow the other car swerved just enough to miss us. John and I sat in silence for a moment. Then we both swore and thanked our lucky stars. I apologised. I hadn't been concentrating. I hadn't 'come down' and my mind was still back in the mortuary. John said he understood and then asked me if I was ok to carry on driving.

I nodded and drove the rest of the way with extreme caution.

When I got home I told Jen about the near miss and about some of the day, without going into too much detail. Although she listened, she didn't seem particularly interested, and couldn't see I might need some sympathy and support. To be fair, I couldn't tell her too much and I'd been going on about DVI ever since I'd been tasked to do the job.

I downed a couple of glasses of wine in an attempt to unwind a bit. Then had a couple more. I started to relax and then realised that the anxiety I had previously felt had completely dissipated. I actually felt elated which seemed entirely wrong to me. I was on a high. In many ways, this had been one of the worst days of my life, so why then did I feel so exhilarated? I couldn't understand it.

I switched the television on to catch the 10.30pm local news. The newsreader was talking about some of the deceased. Images of the young woman, who had such an effect on me, filled the screen. Suddenly a relative or friend was talking about what she was like, what she had achieved in her short life, how she was loved and how she would be missed. I had seen it all in her eyes. She was in my living room. She was everywhere. The incredible rush drained away in a moment and I came crashing back to Earth. A painful lesson for me. From that day, I would recommend 'non-association'. Do not watch or listen to the news or anything likely to make the deceased victims 'real'. Stifling that curiosity is a must, really a matter of self-preservation but – as I would learn – it's much harder to do than you might think. Although totally exhausted, I hardly slept that night. I remember that young woman's name, her job, everything I learned about her. She was the first of the many victims who will remain in my memory forever.

SEVEN
COMING DOWN

The third day started as the second, with our preparations now feeling ritualistic. I was so far pleased with my performance; I'd gone from glorified removal man to advisor and then supervisor, overseeing the completion of the identification forms at every stage of the process. I'd learned so much, and spotted potential for positive change.

There remained little consideration for health and safety and people grew more casual in their dress as time wore on. That morning, when I got changed, putting on the same tyvek suit that I'd worn throughout (unheard of these days), I stopped short of pulling the top half of the suit over my shoulders. I instead tied the arms around my waist so it was only half on. I looked like a cricket umpire. I didn't bother with a mask; neither did anyone else. And we ate our lunch whilst still kitted up.

We started the process again at 8am and again worked solidly through the day. The parts in the body bags were getting smaller, but no matter how small, they were treated just the same in terms of the process, making sure that everything we did was bang on for accurate identification. The last body part was the smallest and we finished at around six in the evening. Victim recovery from the scene was completed in less than forty-eight hours and, overlapping with the recovery procedure, the mortuary took three days to complete the identification process.

I had a massive sense of satisfaction. I knew without doubt that we had identified each and every body and body part correctly, and that the bereaved could now be assured that their loved one could be returned to them for final closure.

I'd now had the 'hands on' experience that I had desperately wanted, and I had passed on my theoretical knowledge to untrained officers 'in the field'. Most of all, I had proved to myself that I could deal with fragmented bodies and was ready to do so time and again, and that I had a lot to offer, as well as a desire to improve the procedures.

Once our job was done, our conclusions, along with ante-mortem data were sent to the reconciliation unit. It is then the job of a team of police officers and other professionals such a fingerprint experts, dentists and forensic scientists to match ante-mortem with post-mortem data. When a match has been established, it is this evidence that is presented to the Identification Commission. The Identification Commission will hear and consider the evidence as to why body or body part number 'x' is thought to belong to that of person 'y'. If enough information and evidence, based on the criteria set has been submitted, HM Coroner will formerly declare the person as deceased and will open and adjourn the inquest. If HM Coroner is not satisfied with the evidence gathered on either the ante- or post-mortem side, then the police are required to obtain further evidence and re-present the case.

For Dunkeswick, a small reconciliation team was formed, which made the comparisons and submitted the evidence to the Identification Commission. I wasn't asked to be involved in any part of the reconciliation process or Identification Commission for Dunkeswick, which sat behind closed doors at the RAF base. The Police Senior Investigating Officer, Lead Pathologist, Lead Family Liaison Co-ordinator, Odontologist and the Police Mortuary Manager Mike I'Hanson formed the Commission, with HM Coroner chairing.

I initially felt disappointed because the steer and reassurance that I provided was never acknowledged. My disappointment was compounded when, a short time after the incident, North Yorkshire Police produced a documentary video about the disaster. It was entitled *A Small Major Disaster* and the Force's staff told their stories of how they had successfully dealt with all aspects of the disaster and took all of the credit for how well they had done. The only acknowledgement of the help they had received, not only from South Yorkshire Police but from many other Forces and agencies, was on the credits at the end of the film. It was just so typical of how the Police Service could never be seen to ask for help. Always fit for purpose, always the consummate professionals and Jack of all Trades. Everyone knows that we can't prepare for every eventuality and asking for help is the most natural thing to do.

Myself, John and Graham had been through hell and had gone far beyond our initial remit to help as lifters and shifters. Our involvement had come at a significant psychological price and to not have that acknowledged was extremely frustrating. Another lesson. I'd always make sure that anyone who helped me got full credit.

North Yorkshire Police stated that all of their officers involved in Dunkeswick received counselling soon after being deployed but we were forgotten. All three of us suffered sleepless nights and dreadful flashbacks. John called me about ten days later and told me we'd been ordered to see occupational health for a debrief session. I said that it was too late, besides I was fine and didn't want to go, but the Assistant Chief Constable insisted. It was another couple of weeks before we could be slotted in to occupational health's appointment book and I went along with even more reluctance than I'd felt initially.

As we walked in, I was overcome by a feeling that we were going to be treated like lepers. I wasn't far wrong. As we tried to take our "seats" on the comfy large beanbags and then struggled up again to help ourselves to tea and coffee, the therapist running the session locked the door. I immediately felt trapped.

This was followed by a complete lack of understanding about what we'd been through and what we'd seen. It had been so long since Dunkeswick that our mental wounds were just about healed. All this session did was to unpick these wounds stitch-by-stitch until they were gaping wide – and then rubbed some salt in them for good measure.

I am a big advocate of debriefs and counselling but this one felt like a tick-in-the-box-type exercise carried out by an inexperienced and naïve individual who closed the door behind us afterwards with a sigh of relief that it was over. It was entirely counter-productive. Again, lesson learned. It was glaringly obvious that any diffusing or debriefing in this line of work should take place before the mind has had time to fully process what it's been a witness to and definitely before the person has found their own way to come to terms with it – their own way might not be the best way, if they turn to alcohol, for example, or 'bottle up' and refuse to talk to anyone about it.

I'm a great believer in ensuring that anyone who has been involved in DVI processes or anything similar should be afforded an individual risk assessment, their personal reactions assessed, and they should be treated according to their needs within 72 hours of returning from a deployment. Group therapy sessions are not the best approach. While the majority of people are okay post-incident, a minority struggle to process the events they've been through. Picking over everything for the strugglers can send the copers back to day one so that they have to start processing the event all over again. Also, although we were of course free to discuss the job in clinical and social environments, it was vital to warn DVI teams to never refer to the victims by name. Care must always be taken not to cause any distress to the bereaved and to maintain the dignity and integrity of those who have perished.

There were no mistakes or hitches at the mortuary for Dunkeswick. The results of the investigation revealed that the pilots were healthy and adequately rested, free of any toxins, that the plane had not been struck by lightning or interfered with by criminal elements. The cause of the crash was a malfunctioning artificial horizon, an instrument used in an aircraft to inform the pilot of the orientation of the aircraft relative to Earth's horizon, used especially in instrument meteorological conditions (IMC), an aviation flight category that describes bad weather conditions that require pilots to fly primarily by reference to instruments, rather than by outside visual references. The commanding pilot became disoriented as he tried to fly through the storm without it and, after attempting to return to the airport, lost control of the plane, which went into a spiral dive. Memorials to the victims can be found at Weeton Church, close to the scene of the crash and at Great Heck, where there is a peace garden.

Our experience generated a hell of a lot of learning. For a start, I knew something had to be done about those blasted Interpol forms. If nothing else, people needed to be trained in their use, so when an incident took place they didn't lead to delays.

I already advocated that we must always afford a body or body part dignity and respect, so covering them post process and re-storing them appropriately became a must for me. My idea of using different coloured body bags came about because of Dunkeswick; in the future one colour would be used at the scene for recovery and pre DVI process and another colour would be used for post-process storage. All labels and paperwork were still to remain with the body or body part throughout. This would mitigate any potential confusion about what stage of the whole process a body or body part was at.

I learned that the actual process proved to be less clinical than I imagined it would be and that improvements in evidential continuity could be made, including considerations around the pathology team doing the strip and search and how this part of the process could be streamlined. Also, the same entire processes were always carried out even though we had already confirmed someone's identity with 100% satisfaction, i.e., through fingerprinting and odontology. I came away from Dunkeswick knowing that the process should be limited to what was actually required for identity on an individual basis rather than having an almost obsessive 'let's do absolutely everything for each body' approach. Once we were 100% sure, then nothing more needed to be done.

I also knew that un-trained staff had to be an absolute no-go in the future. It's not that untrained officers are incapable as they are still consummate professionals, but they are not mentally prepared, which is simply not right. The fingerprint officer I mentioned earlier definitely became a psychological casualty, along with a few others because they were not equipped. I still feel guilty about her now because I knew, I could see it but I didn't do anything about it. Easy with hindsight of course, but I realised that I had seriously under-egged the psychological side, and that I needed to rectify this during training.

I knew post-Dunkeswick that we needed to look at a massive shift in the training we delivered, making the emphasis more about de-selection than selection. We needed to provide the volunteer officers with a real 'warts and all' course allowing them an informed basis on which to make the decision as to whether or not this kind of work was for them.

The one thing that remained unspoken during Dunkeswick, and was in fact a bit of a mystery to me, was the issue of family viewing. The police approach then was to shield the bereaved from seeing their deceased loved one in an almost patronising way, i.e.: "You don't want to see them, love. Just be assured that he/she didn't suffer." I'm really not sure what actually happened at Dunkeswick, but I imagine that the grieving did not get the opportunity to see the remains of their loved ones, even if they'd wished. This played on my mind (particularly in relation to the young lady whose body was intact) and I thought that there must be a way this could be handled better.

Finally, Dunkeswick proved to me that disaster could be dealt with effectively and efficiently outside of the Met Police. There were no boundaries in expertise and experience. I knew that the DVI process that we had been developing needed to be recognised and implemented nationally and, as it turned out, Dunkeswick became the springboard to my getting involved in the national scene and to establish today's Disaster Victim Identification process.

EIGHT

A RECORD-BREAKING

COLLISION

FEBRUARY 28, 2001. 06:12

Caller: *Hello, er, I've had an accident on the M62, I've gone off the road and I'm on an embankment, I'm on a railway line.*

999 Operator: *Oh right, and the vehicle's blocking, still on the railway line.*

Caller: *Yeah the veh, the vehicle's on the railway line, yeah.*

Operator: *Right, okay then, whereabouts on the M62, which carriageway were you travelling on?*

Caller: *I was travelling er, westbound.*

Operator: *Westbound. Where have you gone from and to?*

Caller: *Oh, er, I'm, I'm just, I think I'm near the A1.*

Operator: *You're near the A1 junction?*

Caller: *Yeah, the A1 junction.*

Operator: *Right, how far away, do you know?*

Caller: *Er, no, I wasn't far from the M1, it's just where the A1, just where the, the railway line.*

Operator: *Right, okay, it's just that I'm going to need a better location than that, you're through to North Yorkshire Police here.*

Caller: *But there's a train coming.*
Operator: *Oh my God.*
[Sound of train roaring past]
Caller: *Fucking hell, fucking hell!*
Operator: *Hello?*
Caller: *The train's just gone straight through the front of my Land Rover.*

***

Gary Hart, 36, a divorced father of four, had spent the night playing computer games and talking to Kristeen Panter, a woman he'd met a few days earlier via an Internet dating agency. Hart had fallen for Panter during several hours-long phone conversations over the previous days and they were due to meet for the first time that night.

He'd managed just one hour's sleep in his detached bungalow in the village of Strubby, near Mablethorpe, Lincolnshire, before he got up at 4am. As the boss of his own small building company, Hart liked to be first on site. That morning, he was also planning to deliver a car he'd sold and was towing it on a trailer pulled by his Land Rover on the 145-mile (230km) journey to the building site.

As he joined the M62 Hart drove on autopilot, with one hand on the bottom of the steering wheel (as he later admitted), and had probably drifted off to sleep when he heard a bang come from the back of his car. Hart grabbed the wheel, but the car had already veered off the motorway and he hit a verge, bumped along its ridge and then, as the engine cut out, he slid nose-first down a 45 degree hill coming to a bumpy stop once the ground leveled out. At first, Hart thought he was in a field but his heart jumped when he realized the Land Rover had stalled and was trapped on the East Coast railway mainline, next to the hamlet of Great Heck. The driver's door was jammed, so Hart climbed out of the passenger side and dialed 999 on his mobile phone.

He was twenty feet away from his vehicle and could see the faces of some of the hundred people on board the 04:45 Newcastle to London intercity 225 Great North Eastern Railway electric express train as it rushed past at 125mph and ploughed into his Land Rover.

The express, with the Land Rover held fast at its front by the sheer momentum of the impact, remained upright, travelling for 700 metres, through a set of points, after which a piece of metal broke off the car and hit the lead wheel of the train, causing it to judder and slip its rail, ploughing on regardless at nearly 100mph as it left the tracks.

To the passengers it felt as though the tracks had given away to nothing; the train jumped and bucked in all directions as the out-of-control carriages, free of the rails, hawed and swayed.

The freight train travelling at over 70mph in the opposite direction was twenty minutes ahead of schedule. It was coming from the port of Immingham in Humberside to Ferrybridge in West Yorkshire, carrying about 1,000 tonnes of imported coal in seventeen wagons. The driver hit the brakes but it was too late.

They collided head-on, the express travelling at 70mph and the freight train at around 75mph. The power generated by the impact was equivalent to the detonation of a tonne of TNT. Passengers were plunged into darkness as the train lost power and were catapulted from their seats with some people being hurled the length of carriages. The roof of the express's buffet car was torn off and people were thrown from the train while the front carriage of the freight train slid on its side towards the home of retired power station worker Peter Hintz, 61, who was woken by the sounds of destruction – the train demolishing his garden shed, workshop, summer house and caravan before coming to rest a few feet from his living room.

It was over in seconds. Former railway worker Raymond Brindley came to in the upturned rear carriage, fairly uninjured. After smashing the glass on the emergency door, he clambered out onto a verge. People were screaming. The air was thick with the stink of diesel. He ran, thinking of the injured and the consequences of a possible fire – diesel sparked into life by any number of torn and sparking cables – searching for a lineside telephone. He found one moments later and called the signalman, who was able to bring all other trains on the line to a stop. When Brindley turned and looked back down the tracks he again became conscious of the cries for help, and saw total devastation. All nine carriages of the passenger train were derailed, with one somehow almost completely flattened and another flung into nearby fields. Survivors, the walking wounded, were emerging, stunned, from the wreckage

Twenty-two-year-old Janine Edwards from York had been on her way to an audition for drama school. She came around to the sounds of screams. The lady she'd been seated next to had been flung across the carriage and was trapped under debris. Another woman was screaming that she could feel bone poking through her leg. The man who had been sitting opposite her was streaming with blood, the result of a smashed window cutting into his body. Scenes like this were repeated throughout the length of the express train, which had been subjected to the fastest collision in British rail history.

***

Life since Dunkeswick had not been kind to me. My marriage was failing, thanks in part to my career. I'd moved to Doncaster CID, a very busy division, to take on the role of Detective Inspector there and the job really pushed me to my limit. This meant I spent so much time away from home I was hardly ever there. This remains the sad story of so many police officers, and Jen and I separated in 2001.

The divorce was long, acrimonious and bitter but I'd now met Karon, who supported me 100 per cent during my turmoil. She also showed interest, empathy and sympathy with my work, not just my DVI work, but the demands of my busy day job too. I lost half of my assets and half my police pension in the divorce but ended up with the love of my life, my best friend and my soul mate. We married in 2003 and have never looked back.

Also around this time, I failed a promotion board and, although gutted, if I had succeeded, I would most probably have been assigned a post that would have removed me from the world of DVI. Looking back now, I can see how this event, awful at the time, was in fact one of the best things that ever happened to me.

If this wasn't enough, I also had to endure an operation to remove a prolapsed disc from my back, the result of a police road accident back 1990, which left me with severe whiplash. I'd been in pain for years and couldn't put off the operation any longer. However, the enforced time off gave me time to work on the manual that would form the basis for almost everything we do today in DVI

So, although there were many terrible things for me to endure, I would (eventually) come to realise that all were necessary and in fact had the effect of improving my life enormously.

I was just back at work, still recuperating and still going through my divorce, when I got the call. A train collision near Selby, multiple fatalities, number unknown. I was needed to advise on recovery of the deceased and then set up and operate a temporary mortuary. Suddenly here I was, six years after Dunkeswick with a chance to see how well my ideas for recovery and identification would work. And my superiors would be watching to see how well I performed.

I waited until I had the all-clear from the emergency services, that the wounded had been removed and then hit the road.

I was scared and apprehensive, and spent the journey wondering whether I would be able to hack it.

It didn't start well. This was before the era of satellite navigation systems and finding a route to the scene was hard enough but getting access was a nightmare. I ditched my car at the end of a dirt road and walked a quarter of a mile to the first of four cordons. No one asked me for my warrant card until I reached the innermost cordon.

Then I spotted photographers were on a bridge overlooking the site. The press were all over it, in prime position to see everything that was going on. I couldn't believe (especially considering it was five hours after the crash) that we'd allowed every man and his dog access to that bridge so they could gawp at and photograph the scene.

The emergency services had arrived fifteen minutes after the accident and the injured had been cleared from the immediate site, with some being treated in a nearby barn until they could be taken to hospital. There were over eighty injuries, many of them serious. A fleet of ambulances, two RAF Sea King helicopters and a West Yorkshire air ambulance helicopter had taken them to six different hospitals.

I searched for the incident's Senior Investigating Officer, Detective Superintendent Nick Bracken. Nick, who was from the British Transport Police, was MDAT-trained and had been the lead investigator into the Paddington Rail Crash in October 1999, which had left 31 people dead. I was reassured that Nick was in charge, he was strong-willed and confident, a natural leader. At the same time, I was a bit concerned that I was unable to find him. I was also concerned about just how chaotic things were. People were tramping through the crash site anyway they liked. This was supposed to be a crime scene, to be treated as a suspected homicide until we found otherwise, with set routes in and out of the area and every person's movement carefully logged. The amount of contamination worried me. While I understood that it must have been utterly overwhelming for the first responders from North Yorkshire Police, which had sparse resources to deal with something on this scale, it was about time this scene was brought under control. I was trying to call Nick and had reached his staff officer but the scene was so noisy that we couldn't hear and in the end we walked into one another while we were still yelling at each other on the phone.

Nick took to me see the Chief Fire Officer who led us on a tour of the site. My hands were shaking from the adrenaline as my mind raced with thoughts of what needed to be done.

"The injured have all been removed," Nick said. "And we have the locations of seven bodies so far. We suspect there might be as many as thirteen dead. There are multiple body parts, upwards of ten so far."

"Any bodies or body parts removed or moved?"

"The Fire Service moved two bodies to the barn because they would have been exposed to the press."

"We need to clear the media from that bridge now," I added.

"Agreed, I'll sort it."

"And what about access to the bodies?" I asked.

"Some more difficult than others," the Chief Fire Officer replied, "But we have equipment that can deal with that once you've had a chance to examine them."

Even though I was now familiar with crash sites, I had never seen carnage on this scale. I took a long moment to stare at a first-class carriage, flattened by a fully loaded coal-carrier that had somehow managed to roll over it and was still partially covering one end.

We had to climb through wreckage to find the victims, at one point we passed below a carriage that was half-hanging off the track, finely balanced at an angle of 45 degrees. No health and safety here.

"We'll need cranes at some point," the CFO added before asking me where we planned to take the bodies.

"Regular hospital and public mortuaries won't be able to cope, so we'll take them to RAF Linton-on-Ouse. I'll clear this with the Coroner."

This was over thirty miles away from the crash site, but just a few miles from York, from where the Coroner and dozens of additional mortuary staff would come.

The fire chief showed me the bodies and parts they'd found so far, some trapped under carriages. Huge chunks of wreckage were unrecognisable as once belonging to a train.

"You're the expert," the CFO said once we'd finished our walk-through. "So where do you want to start?"

I didn't feel like one. I felt as though this was a challenge beyond my capabilities. My job was to examine and recover the bodies in a dignified manner, I told myself, and that I had established a process for this.

The recommended procedure for an incident of this type is to first rescue the living and clear access to and from the site, as well as rescuing the trapped and injured. Next is to recover the human remains, before facilitating any criminal investigations. Body recovery was now top priority and that meant I needed to crack on. Personal items and technical items of evidential value would be moved last, once the Nick was satisfied that they could be moved.

Eventually, during my second, more detailed walk-through, my professionalism kicked in and I started to fire out orders and make calls. I established routes in and out of the scene and estimated (with the help of the CFO) that we'd need three days to search the entire scene and the length of both trains to complete the recovery of every last body part.

The carriages would have to be photographed before we lifted them. We'd need photography of body parts, bodies and possessions that might help ID victims. Every body part would have its own Unique Reference Number (URN), no matter how small, and would be treated separate from any body, even if they were lying right next to a body and may match in the most obvious way. I was determined not to make a mistake, for the families' sakes.

I looked out across farmland, saw cows in the fields and a barn in the distance. I approached the fire officer.

"You said the injured were treated in a barn."

"That's right."

"We're in the middle of a foot-and-mouth crisis," I said, "We're going to need to disinfect everything and everyone that comes and goes."

To start with we needed to improve the cordons, keeping the inner cordon to a single access point for the recovery team while the command team ran the operation from the secondary cordon, including the SERM (Scene Evidence Recovery Manager) as well as fire, ambulance, representatives from the local authority and any specialist advisers, in this case engineers from the rail and utilities companies. We established safe routes in and out using temporary walkways – known as forensic pathways. Everyone entering and leaving the inner cordon would be logged in and out. The bridge overlooking the crash site was closed and a Media Liaison Post was set up on the very edge of the outer cordon.

We also needed a team in the much larger secondary cordon to marshal all the vehicles from the police services, the Coroner, as well as engineers from the rail and utility companies, not to mention the Ministry of Agriculture Fisheries and Food (MAFF).

Martin Hemmingway, then a Chief Inspector and trained DVI operative from South Yorkshire Police, was brought in to oversee the recovery operation along with DVI-trained staff, also from South Yorks, and the British Transport Police. We then established a body holding area on the outside edge of the inner cordon and a property audit area beyond this. We would need to have an overview of both of these areas and would also oversee the recovery of bodies and body parts, confirming that the process was handled well and everything recorded correctly. Martin had been on one of my DVI courses and had been deployed in Kosovo in 1997 to assist with identifying the victims of war crimes. A SIO (Senior Investigating Officer) would concentrate on gathering evidence but procedure correctly dictated that the recovery of the victims' bodies took precedent.

The recovery team quickly grew until we eventually numbered 35 police officers and 25 specialist officers, including the property recovery coordinator, the Police Search Adviser (PolSA), the Forensic Co-ordinator and a dozen search-trained officers.

Most people brought their own colour-coordinated gear (we wore white boiler suits and reflective yellow tabards) but we made sure we had plenty of extras. We had extra head protection, facemasks, eye protectors, disposable suits, gloves, safety wellingtons, torches, ID armbands, backpacks and multi-purpose tools. We also had body and viscera bags and decontamination equipment including buckets, bowls, water, cleaning fluids, chairs, tables, matting, antiseptic wipes and disinfectant "boot baths". Decontamination areas were set up and the disposal of contaminated clothing was performed to MAFF's requirements.

There were plenty of hazards for us to worry about. Some of the wreckage was unstable and the location of some of the human remains meant we had to move very carefully, for our safety, as well as to try and best preserve the bodies as we found them. We also had to remain mindful of the hazards that come from toxic smoke and dust, the risk of electrocution from damaged cables, gas explosion from ruptured mains/tanks and fuel fumes and what the trains might have been transporting – trains are used to carry nuclear waste, for example. In this case, the freight train had been carrying a hundred tonnes of coal and there was 3,000 gallons of spilt fuel, so we needed to be aware of the risk of fire, although the Fire Service did a terrific job neutralising the diesel. We established emergency evacuation procedures for rescue teams should the worst happen.

Of course, psychological stress is also a major factor for rescue teams. Rest areas were established, out of view of the crash site so that people could take a moment, have a cup of tea and talk with colleagues. A major cause of that stress was the occasional sound of a mobile phone ringing from within the carriages. A loved one who had just heard about the crash? A work colleague wondering why they hadn't shown up for a meeting? You just have to push these thoughts aside. The key to making it through each incident as psychologically unscathed as possible was to focus on the job.

A doctor accompanied recovery teams to officially pronounce each person as 'life extinct' and photographs of each body were taken before we touched them. And this was only after we had permission from the Coroner, who had official responsibility for the bodies until they were handed over to the families or more specifically, their choice of funeral director. The only exception is if the body is in danger of destruction or blocking the path to a live victim. The Coroner has legal jurisdiction over the bodies but cannot own them. A deceased person cannot be property.

In this case, the Coroner was David Hinchliffe from West Yorkshire. David was an obvious choice as he'd worked on the Dunkeswick air crash. David appointed Professor Chris Milroy from The Medico Legal Centre in Sheffield as supervising Forensic Pathologist. I knew Chris well and had sought his advice in developing the DVI protocols. I informed them that we would need to activate the Temporary Mortuary Plan. This is a big decision, as it's an expensive logistical nightmare. Apart from the fact we had more fatalities than regular mortuaries could cope with, this was an 'Open Incident', i.e., there was no passenger manifest, so we could not predict the number of dead that might be trapped under railway carriages that might take days to search, or know their identities in advance.

Everything, every decision and action, with reasons, was written down as we plotted the position of each body and part (using a GPS locator). We took photos, labelled fragments and each was given its own URN. The bodies were labelled and the labels were attached to the upper arm, wherever possible. A copy of the label was also fastened to the exterior of the body bags. Once all this was done we lifted and carefully placed the body or parts in a body bag where another photo was taken before we zipped and sealed the bag and the body was removed to the holding area, where the holding officer would check and sign the paperwork. Body parts were placed in smaller opaque bags.

Bodies are not searched at the scene. A systematic and detailed search would take place by trained and equipped officers in the sterile environment of the mortuary. We simply performed an Initial Visual Check (IVC) to locate any obvious material to help with identification, from a lanyard or ID badge to a tattoo or distinctive jewellery. The IVC is restricted to what we can see without moving or exploring clothing etc. Any useful information from the IVC is immediately logged. Any personal items found next to a body are also photographed, their locations marked and then the objects are bagged and fastened to the body.

The process cannot be rushed. One has to think of safety, accuracy and the integrity of the evidence. It took seven days, more than double the time I first predicted, to complete the search of the scene. We needed heavy cranes to lift carriages into a position where they could be systematically searched. Attention to detail was everything; the smallest body part of the 46 body parts we recovered was a human tooth. During this time, the villagers in Great Heck had, with the help of police officers, laid wreaths and flowers on the bridge above the crash site, directly above the derailed second wagon of the coal train and the last coach of the doomed express.

The weather was cold but dry, which helped with the aerial photography. This had to be completed before we started to move carriages and other debris, which would be transported to secure locations for further study. It was quite possible that more, albeit small, human remains would be contained somewhere within the larger pieces of wreckage. It was impossible to look inside a few of the small voids among the twisted metal, and although we carefully swept the train four times using sound and thermal detectors, we couldn't be certain we had everything.

The village had changed dramatically in that bulldozers dug away part of the local Bridgeside Nurseries' garden and two paddocks to double, overnight, the number of roads in the railway hamlet allowing heavy lifting tenders to take crane parts for assembly by the tracks.

I was worried about finding more bodies in the wreckage of the flattened first class carriage, and in the chaos of broken wheels and undercarriage below another first class carriage and the buffet car, but once the cranes had hoisted the unstable pyramid of coaches out of the way, and after police dogs failed to find any human remains we might have missed, we knew we had a total of ten deceased, all male.

NINE

EMOTIONAL MOMENTS

As my focus shifted to the mortuary, it seemed as though everywhere I turned someone was asking me what to do next, saying things like "you're the expert", "the font of all knowledge" and "the answer to our prayers". I know these statements were meant well, but they just added to pressure and made me feel slightly annoyed. I had more experience than most of disasters but that was all. No matter what you've been through before, every disaster is a unique situation and we all have to adapt.

Chief Inspector Howard Harding, another Dunkeswick veteran, was in charge of the mortuary operation. Realising how valuable experience was, Howard brought the same team that had worked in the mortuary for the Dunkeswick crash.

The bodies were carefully transported under the supervision of the records officer, just in case anything was dropped or knocked, so that we knew every possible incident had been noted. Once the body bags arrived, they were inspected to ensure that the labels were correctly filled out and that the bags themselves were still correctly sealed.

Then they entered a conveyor-belt system, where each body and part goes through the examination process in turn. The idea of the examination is to obtain evidence that can be matched with ante-mortem data, collected by specialist officers from the homes and/or workplaces of people who'd been reported missing.

Two storage areas had been set aside, for pre- and post-mortem, and different coloured body bags were used. Each body bag was opened on the mortuary tray. Depending on the state of the remains, it's sometimes easier to leave the contents in the body bag. A plastic hospital ID bracelet is placed on the victim's wrist, if possible, and labelled with an ID number. Next, photographs of the clothed body are taken from the front, back and side. An instant photo is also taken at this point, and attached to the victim's file.

Then all jewellery, watches, wallets, documentation are removed from body, labelled, examined, described (noting if it's bloodstained) and photographed. If an item is wet or damp, it may not be best to seal it in a plastic evidence bag. The exhibits officer has the final say on item storage.

This process is one of the hardest parts of the job for me, because this is the point where it's impossible to keep the body separate from the person. As soon as you go through a victim's pockets, their lives open up in your hand. You see their driving license, bankcards, cinema tickets; a photo of their wife, mother and father, kids... They were enjoying life, thinking they had a future – before you know it you're emotionally involved at a deep level.

I trained people to treat the deceased with dignity and respect and this meant remaining professional at all times – which is easier said than done. To achieve this, I usually suggest they try and distance themselves from the victim as a person. Respect them but don't try to get to know them or their families. The job we have to do is hard enough as it is. The victims remain anonymous and are allocated a code instead of a name, until formal identification is made to help with this. We are human of course, and this tactic will only go so far. As we went through their pockets, our thoughts turned to their families and our own families, trying to imagine what it would be like for our own loved ones to go through this, what it must be like to experience this sudden and utterly undeserved loss.

We were in the process of searching and undressing a victim when his mobile phone, which was in his trouser pocket, rang. The device's ring was so eerie that we all froze for a moment. The techies tell us that the best thing for us to do is to turn off any mobile phones when we find them but, to prevent losing data by pushing the wrong button or swiping the screen incorrectly, we keep a supply of aluminium Faraday Bags, which prevent any signal being emitted or received by a device. I saw the phone's screen as I removed it from the man's pocket. The display said MUM. We let the rings finish and then placed the phone in a Faraday Bag.

We never make the assumption that property found next to a body belonged to that person. It might have come from someone nearby who was injured, or be dropped by a suspect, or even from a member of the rescue team. All is chaos in the wake of a mass fatality accident but it's sometimes easy to forget this in the stillness of a cleared scene.

Property is divided into:

Group One: items that can be directly matched to a person, such as passports, bank cards, mobile phones and unique jewellery.

Group Two: items such as books and paperwork, toys.

All property is cleaned before being returned to the next of kin, except in the case of faiths that require all parts of the body to be cremated or buried, and therefore includes bloodstained clothing. A new photograph is taken of each item before it's returned.

Once the items are logged the body is undressed and all details of the clothing are labelled, described, photographed and stored. The body is then washed and a physical description is made, noting any scars, malformations, amputations, etc., and is photographed front and back.

A radiographer then scans the body, looking for any surgical appliances, pathologies, healed fractures and unique bone structures. Oral radiography is also performed for dental records. Prints are taken of the fingers, palm, toes and feet. Details of any missing fingers and toes are recorded.

Once the initial examination is complete, the pathologist performs a post-mortem to establish cause of death. Finally, the remains of each person are placed into a new bag. Original soiled bags may be of some evidential value so these are themselves bagged, sealed and treated as exhibits.

This was the first incident in the UK where DNA was used throughout the DVI process and we used the results to successfully match all the body parts.

A separate room near the camp chapel, about thirty metres from the mortuary hangar, with all religious symbols and items removed, was used for viewing. A Viewing Officer supervised the process, once the identity of the victim had been confirmed. To help this process, the Coroner will sometimes use reconstructive techniques. Family liaison officers (FLOs) accompanied the families at all times. Viewing complete, the body is prepared for release to family members.

Throughout the examination and identification process we stayed on site. Going home to your family during in an operation like this – which lasted ten days – only adds to the stress. It's not fair to burden our families with late night horror stories, or to try and protect them by bottling up our memories. On site, we can debrief and talk openly with our workmates, who know exactly what we've been through and who are likely to be feeling the same way.

The mortuary is a quiet place, which is surprising because a great many people are involved. The key people are the Mortuary Operations manager (now Police Mortuary Operations

Coordinator), a senior police officer responsible for all police operations in the mortuary and the Senior Identification Manager, responsible for all the police staff involved in all aspects of the identification process. There are also post-mortem fingerprint officers (who also take footprints and ear prints), the mortuary documentation manager, mortuary facilities manager, forensic pathologists, mortuary loggists, body reception officers, body storage officers, post mortem document officers, exhibits officers, body search officers, forensic odontologists, forensic anthropologists, mortuary photographers, stretcher bearers, and a first aider, along with various ancillary staff.

When deceased victims or human remains are not being subjected to a particular mortuary process they must be kept in a refrigerated area for safe storage. Bodies are kept at four degrees Centigrade, which will preserve them for examination for up to 28 days. Long-term storage requires bodies to be stored between -15 and -20 degrees Centigrade.

During the Selby operation we needed an additional refrigeration unit, one-metre long, in which to store body parts. When the delivery arrived, I raised the hangar doors and guided the articulated lorry in. Once in place, I signalled for driver to stop and went to meet him at the front. The side door was already open and he was stepping down as I approached.

And then he stopped.

We had some old-fashioned hospital screens set up at the start of the mortuary for privacy. A token effort, which really didn't do much to obscure what was going on behind them. From his elevated position, the driver was able to look down the examination line and saw the large number of victims and parts being examined at every stage of the process. His faced turned ashen. That look will stay with me forever. He was a young man, in his late twenties, and clearly he'd never seen anything of the sort and probably never would ever again.

I tried to get him to jump down but he'd frozen. My adrenaline was working overtime thanks to my blunder and so I reached up and practically lifted him to the ground. I turned him so we were face-to-face and he seemed to come round, although his skin was as white as my Tyvek suit.

"Are you okay?" I asked.

He nodded, shakily, after a moment. "Yeah, fine. Don't worry about it." He walked around to the back of the lorry, opened up, unhitched the load, brought it onto the loading platform and wheeled it onto the ground. He looked like he was on autopilot.

I fussed over him a bit too much, partly out of concern for him but mainly because I could see a claim coming. I tried to make out as though he hadn't seen what he had seen.

"Would you like a tea?" I asked, hoping to win him over with a cuppa.

He looked at me like I was mad. Why would anyone want to hang around here a second longer than they needed to? He politely refused, climbed back into his cab and was on his way seconds later. I worried for months afterwards that a complaint and/or claim would come but it never did. This was a massive lesson for me and while it might not be much of a consolation to that poor lorry driver, I've never repeated this mistake. I was left with horrifying flashbacks for months after this job and I wondered if the experience, however fleeting, was enough to give the young driver the same kind of nightmares.

The identification process took about three days of the fifty-strong team working twelve-hour shifts. We spent a total ten days in the mortuary, matching body parts and possessions to victims, cleaning and returning items.

Once we were done, ten separate funeral hearses arrived and drove the bodies out in slow procession, a tough emotional moment for us all.

The ten men who died were:

John Weddle, 47, from Throckley, the driver of the express train. John, a father-of-two, had worked on the railways for 26 years. A memorial plaque has since been placed at Newcastle Station, near his home, which features a guitar – he was a keen musician – as well as GNER's logo

Stephen Dunn, 29, from Brayton, the driver of the coal train. His son James was nine-years-old at the time and today drives London Underground engineering trains. "My dad died doing a job he truly loved," James said, "A job he considered a paid hobby."

Raymond Robson, 43, from Whitley Bay was the express train guard. He had 24 years of rail service and saved the life of a man in 1998, bringing a train to a stop in time to prevent a would-be-suicide at Peterborough Station.

Paul Taylor, 42 from Newcastle had just been awarded the title of GNER Chef of the Year. Paul lived with Lee – his wife of 17 years – and their two children at their home in Longbenton in Newcastle.

Alan Ensor, 44, from York, was a civil engineering project manager and father of two sons, aged eleven and 13.

Clive Vidgen, 39, from York had worked for the railways for 22 years, following in the footsteps of his father, a rail linesman, who was killed by a train near York in December 1969 while repairing track.

Steve Baldwin, 44, from York. Professor Baldwin made fateful changes to his travel plans after he was invited by the Institute of Psychiatry to talk about his work with children diagnosed with Attention Deficit Hyperactivity Disorder (ADHD). He decided to take the early train at the last minute, so he would have time to prepare his speech about what he called the "quick fix" of drugging children diagnosed with ADHD. Years of research that was bringing new hope to hundreds of parents with children diagnosed with ADHD, died with him.

Christopher Terry, 30, from York, was travelling to London for a job interview. The computer expert was hoping this new job would allow him to see more of his wife and young son Benedict.

Robert Shakespeare, 43, from Beverley. Robert, the father of four children aged nine to seventeen, was an IT manager and print colour management specialist. Robert normally worked from home but had to travel to London for a business meeting.

Barry Needham, 40, from York. A freight logistics coordinator, it was Barry's day off but he'd decided to travel to Doncaster to help out with an emergency at work. A few days before the tragedy, Barry's wife Margitta asked Robert what he would like for his birthday. He replied: "Just for us to be together".

***

It was a great relief when we were able to stand down. We had completed a safe recovery, accurate identification and return of the bodies to their families. Our desire to do what was best for the families, along with our attention to detail had got us through a tough process. More than one of these officers had shed tears during the operation.

An RAF chaplain was on duty throughout. She was supportive and came to visit us in the mortuary once or twice a day. When I told the chaplain, after three days, that ten of the South Yorkshire staff were being released, as most of the examinations had been completed, she asked if she could come to the mortuary and address them in the rest room to thank them for their efforts. This sounded like a good idea to me, and I appreciated the thought.

My first mistake to was to introduce the Chaplain as the 'Camp Vicar', which caused a few titters, but I was so caught up in the seriousness of the moment that I didn't notice until someone explained it to me later. She began by saying many kind words about the importance of our work and the respect with which we'd carried it out. Then she asked us to bow our heads.

"I'd like you to now take a few minutes to pause in silence and for you to think about the victims of this disaster and to give thoughts to the loved ones they will leave behind."

She continued in the same vein, trying to make us focus on everything I always said that we shouldn't think about.

I started to sweat as I took in the words. I wanted it over as soon as possible but I just couldn't bring myself to interrupt the vicar. I froze. Her words had already taken affect and I couldn't move. The best I could manage was to wait for just twenty seconds after she had finished speaking and then break the silence by thanking her. The others were in a similar state, almost trance-like. I could see tears streaming down cheeks. We practically collapsed when the Chaplain left. I should have briefed her beforehand. A mistake never to be repeated.

I admitted my failings during the debrief session and tried to bring the team back to a point where they could congratulate themselves on a difficult job well done and bury any demons awakened by the well-meaning chaplain.

***

Gary Hart was jailed for five years for causing the disaster. Released after thirty months, he started a new life in South Wales, where in 2011, on the tenth anniversary of the crash, he gave an interview to a Welsh radio station. In the interview he blamed "fate" for the crash.

His comments came as families and friends of victims, rail staff and emergency crews gathered for memorial services for the crash – described by the judge who jailed Hart as the worst caused by a driver in the UK in modern times.

Hart said: "There's not a day gone by that I haven't thought about Selby. There's an awful lot of guilt attached with the accident. I do feel for the families because it was a horrendous, horrible way to go, to die ... I was nearly there myself. I know nothing about them. I've absolved myself not of responsibility, but of knowing anything about them. That would degenerate my life into misery ... I survived this accident and I want to survive the rest of my life and remain sane in some way."

* * *

As far as my DVI procedures were concerned, Selby was a success and a short time later I was offered a secondment to Centrex (the Central Police Training and Development Authority) where I would design, develop and deliver DVI training to a hundred Senior Investigation Officers across the UK so they could perform the role of Senior Identification Manager (SIM).

The role of SIM was the result of one of the 36 recommendations made by the non-statutory public enquiry into the investigation into the identification of victims of transport incidents, presided over by Lord Justice Clarke. Lord Justice Clarke had been commissioned specifically to look into the events that followed the Thames River Boat disaster of August 1989, when 51 young people lost their lives[2]. The findings were aimed at providing more care, support and information to families in DVI scenarios, and the recommendations reflected this. Recommendation Ten stated that after a mass fatality incident, the Police should appoint a second SIO to oversee the identification aspect of the enquiry. He/she would work alongside the other SIO who investigated the case for cause and criminal liability. The idea of the

---

2   See page 147 for a full account of the inquiry and the families' incredibly difficult journey for truth and justice

second SIO was to accurately expedite the identification process, shortening the wait of families whose relatives had perished.

In conceding that he couldn't be prescriptive on how the authorities dealt with every mass fatality incident, Lord Justice Clarke issued four principles which authorities involved in any aspect of DVI should adhere to:

Honest and accurate information to families at all times

A sympathetic and caring approach to families and the bereaved

Respect for the deceased and the bereaved

The avoidance at all costs, of mistaken identification[3]

Apply the HART principles to any aspect of DVI planning and you won't go far wrong. These principles run through all my work like 'Blackpool' runs through a stick of rock.

Lord Justice Clarke's findings were published in March 2001, just after Selby and they proved to be my gateway to working on DVI at a national level. It also gave me a chance to roll out my DVI training on a national level in the hope that it would become accredited.

I joined Centrex in January 2003, knowing I was scheduled to retire in 2006. While this was plenty of time for me to create a national training system and to get hundreds, if not thousands, of people trained in DVI and disaster response, I was keen to get things in place as soon as possible, as disasters wait for no man. I didn't want to find myself saying 'I'm not ready,' when the time came, for it is always a question of 'when' not 'if'.

Sure enough, just as everything was coming together, we entered the year of disaster.

---

3   The fact that the acronym of this mnemonic is HART is pure coincidence and has nothing to do with Gary Hart

TEN

THE LOST SOULS

Morecambe Bay in Lancashire, at 300 km², is the largest bay of its kind in the UK. Made up of sand and mud tidal flats, the area is extremely treacherous with 10metre high tides that can overtake a running man – if he is not first consumed by quicksand. Despite these dangers, and for hundreds of years, fishermen have ventured out onto the shifting sands in search of cockles, a hunt that continues to this day, part of the race for a share of the £8million these edible marine bivalves bring in every year.

Cockles, a small shellfish delicacy, preserved and eaten in vinegar, are popular on the European mainland but thanks to declining numbers, prices have risen enormously and Morecambe has some of the finest cockle beds in Europe. They live just below the sand in clusters of thousands, up to eight miles from the shore. To get to the shellfish, cocklers have to rake the sands and can only do this when the tide is out.

Cocklers are only permitted to work with licenses issued by the local fisheries association. They're paid piecework: the more they collect, the more they earn. They are towed out by tractor-trailer at low tide, and back again before the tides, hidden at first by deep channels that will first cut unwary people off from the shore. Once these channels fill, the sea will cover an acre of sand in just a few minutes, and continue to rise until the several metres deep.

***

I started 2004 fighting fit. My divorce was finalised in 2002. Karon and I had married and I had two beautiful step-daughters, Nicola, 20 and Laura, 16. Since Selby I'd worked as hard as possible on introducing the principles of the findings of the Lord justice Clarke enquiry into DVI and teaching as many people as I could and, as a member of the Major Disaster Advisory Team (MDAT), I was on standby to respond to any mass fatality incident in the UK.[4]

The only fly in the ointment was that Centrex – my base of operations – was located at Bramshill House, a Jacobean mansion in Hampshire owned by the police since 1960. It was 210 miles from home, and made things difficult in terms of spending time with Karon, whose life was in Yorkshire. However, I was at last getting paid to work full time on my passion and memories of my time at the Fraud Squad faded fast as I threw myself into my work, starting at 7.30am and finishing at 6.30pm Monday-Friday as I started to go beyond DVI into all aspects of disaster management. After a short while at Bramshill, however, I was allowed to work from home.

I still didn't feel like I was experienced enough for this role as I'd only worked through two disasters and certainly didn't feel like an expert, although I was by then delivering five-day training courses across the UK to police officers who would become Senior Identification Managers (SIMs). By the end of 2003, I had

---

4   Bramshill House was sold off in 2013 and Centrex was replaced by the National Policing Improvement Agency (NPIA) on 1 April 2007

trained sixty SIMs with many more planned for 2004 – the year I would come to know as the year of disaster.

I was awoken at 6am on 5 February 2004 and ordered to Morecambe Bay. A large group of workers, who were collecting cockles at low tide on sand flats at Warton Sands, near Hest Bank, had been cut off by the incoming tide at around 9:30 pm.

A rescue operation had been launched after one of the cocklers called 999 and screamed at the operator: "Sinking water, many many, sinking water… Sinking water, sinking water."

The caller did not speak much English and was unable to tell the operator anything about where they were before being overcome by the sea. The call was distressing enough to hear afterwards, I can't imagine how hard it must have been for the operator to try and deal with. We later found out that another victim called his wife in China, saying he was in great danger.

Morecambe's RNLI crew, along with local fishermen who volunteered their boats, worked 22 hours straight, first looking for survivors, then bodies. More than forty cocklers were working that night. No one could survive for long before being overcome by hypothermia. Michael Guy, lifeboat operations manager, said that they suddenly "came into a sea of bodies… It was very harrowing. Apart from the senior hovercraft commander, many of the crew… hadn't seen bodies in the water before… So it had a lasting effect on them."

Local fisherman Harold Benson had rushed to help but ended up pulling bodies out of the sea. "I've been on those sands man and boy," he said afterwards. "What happened that night was not only awful beyond words – it was absolutely avoidable… Even when the tide hit them, had they had anybody with them, like me, who knows the area, there was still a safe route off the cockle bed… They could have walked to safety."

By the time I arrived in Morecambe nine bodies had been recovered. They had been placed in the mortuary at the Royal

Lancaster Infirmary. To my surprise, they were all naked. I was appalled to learn that police officers had already undressed them – this was against recognised victim recovery procedures – and Association of Chief Police Officers (ACPO) Victim Labels had not been completed. Victim Labels were introduced in the 1980s. They provide each victim with a Unique Reference Number (URN) that identifies both the victim and the police force dealing with the associated investigation. Each police force has its own number (South Yorkshire's was 33) and this was followed by a consecutive number, so 33001, 33002, and so on. One label would be attached to the body, one would be attached to the bag, one would be left at the scene as a marker for the point of recovery and one was a used a receipt that the recovering officer would hand in to the person in charge of auditing activity at the scene, running the Audit Control Area (now known as the Victim Audit Holding Area), a temporary holding area at the scene for recovered bodies before they were transported to the designated mortuary. These labels also allowed the recovering officer to record brief details of their find and recovery procedure and were therefore extremely helpful for the mortuary teams, providing them with sometimes crucial information before the body bags were opened.

No one in Lancashire was DVI-trained, so detectives started to arrive 'cold' at the mortuary, just by the fact that they were on duty. Some of them had come from Lancaster Police Station where more than a dozen survivors were camped out on an office floor before they were eventually taken to a police accommodation block.

The criminal investigation was already under way and was under the command of Senior Investigation Officer (SIO) Mick Gradwell who appointed newly-trained DCI Steve Brunskill as the Senior Identification Manager (SIM). Steve was the first SIM to perform the role after Lord Justice Clarke's review of

DVI procedures was published. Twenty-five officers, designated to work on DVI, were there by the time I arrived and I briefed them, along with Steve Brunksill, and Alison Armour, the lead home office pathologist, describing the mortuary procedures they would be expected to perform. All of them said they were willing to learn from me on the hoof.

By the time we started, we had nineteen victims, seventeen men and two women, all Chinese and aged somewhere between eighteen and 45. Their bodies were recovered quickly and therefore intact, unusual for a mass fatality incident.

It's a myth that autopsies ID victims. A mortuary examination will only provide evidence as to cause of death.

In other words: Give me a body and I will, with the help of specialists provide you with a DNA profile, dental charting, a set of fingerprints (assuming the fingers are intact and have been recovered), a list of marks, scars, tattoos on the body, a head and shoulders photograph (assuming the person is visually identifiable) and a full list and details of their clothing and personal effects. None of these scientific identifiers can be used to categorically establish the victim's identity. This includes personal ID found in their pockets. Suppose the victim found a wallet earlier that day? Or perhaps a non-DVI-trained police officer picked up a wallet that he found near a victim and put it in the body bag. Perhaps they are carrying a relative's driving license or passport for some bureaucratic reason. All these scenarios have taken place. To satisfy the Coroner, there has to be a successful match between ante mortem and post mortem data.

The two pathologists, although experts in their own right, certainly didn't know about DVI and I didn't expect them to at this time. Identification is an issue for routine autopsy, but it is not normally a problem as these involve individuals who have died at home, in hospital, in car accidents, making them relatively easy to identify. It's a different story with mass fatality incidents that take place in challenging locations especially an incident like the one at Morecambe that involved foreign nationals.

The Coroner decided that DNA, fingerprints, odontology, or a unique medical condition (UMC) would be used to confirm identity. Because this was a criminal investigation, full post-mortems would take place to establish cause of death.

We decided to examine the victims where they were. It was the weekend and the bodies were already in the Royal Lancaster, so we could work through until Monday without interrupting the mortuary's normal routine.

As more bodies continued to arrive, it was decided to recruit another Home Office pathologist, Paul Johnson, to assist Alison. Despite the large numbers, two teams, consisting of a patholo-gist, anatomical pathology technologist, scribe, exhibits officers, photographers, and fingerprint staff were able to work simulta-neously and comfortably in the space available.

It was an exceptionally unusual operation. Although the bodies were in good condition there was little by way of iden-tification. As this investigation involved Chinese nationals and would depend on the assistance of the Chinese authorities, it was decided that we would use the blasted Interpol forms, which were, despite being incredibly and unnecessarily complex and unwieldy, internationally recognised, and therefore made sense as identification of the victims would depend on our successful interaction with the Chinese authorities.

We photographed each victim with the bag that contained their clothing, and then each item in the bag was removed and photographed, along with personal effects (wallets, watches and jewellery), labelled and rebagged according as per recog-nised victim recovery procedures. Luckily, victims and bags had been stored in the same refrigerated compartments. Some of the naked victims did not have any bags of clothing I was told that this was because they had removed them before trying to swim to shore.

In summary then, we ended up with 21 victims to process (a 22nd body was found in autumn 2010, and a 23rd was never found) and they went through the following mortuary procedure:

- Full facial digital and 35mm photographs
- Full body 35mm photographs
- Clothing and personal items photographed and exhibited individually by the Home Office pathologist and police exhibits team
- Interpol DVI forms completed, detailing all visible physical features and descriptions of clothing
- Full sets of fingerprints and footprints (footprints are sometimes used to match prints left on laminate floors, scales, etc.) were taken by Lancashire police's fingerprints bureau staff
- Fingerprints quick-scanned by a team of UK immigration service officers
- Full Home Office standard post mortem examination carried out to determine cause of death
- Blood samples taken so a full DNA profile could be obtained, as well as for toxicology screening.

The cause of death in all cases was drowning after being overcome with hypothermia. Some had died while trying to swim to shore, while four of the victims stayed with the truck they'd used to reach the cockling area. They drowned after it was overcome with water.

The task of identifying the recovered victims as well as two missing individuals, all of Chinese origin, seemed near impossible, especially as it was thought they had entered the UK illegally (there are currently 1.3 billion Chinese people on the planet). Not wanting to be identified, they carried false ID or no ID whatsoever. One of the only clues came when we found a Chinese phone number sewn into the hem of one man's jeans. Another man had a picture of him with his family. These personal items really brought it home to me. These were young and healthy immigrant workers who had endured goodness-only-knows-what to get here, a land of hope, a land that was supposed to free their families of poverty but in reality left them in slavery to the co-called snakehead gangs who charged fortunes to get them to the UK. And then they'd been sent out in the dark – intimidated by their bosses – to shovel cockles in life threatening conditions, without lifejackets, flares, or beacons, all for £5 for every 25kg sack they filled. It was understandable that the survivors didn't want to talk. They were frightened of us but they were more frightened of the cockling bosses and the Snakehead gangs who had started to bring the immigrants to Morecambe in 2003, as the trade took off. They'd also suffered intimidation from rival gangs. Competition was fierce with cockle wars having already taken place between Scottish and Welsh rivals and the arrival of the cheap Chinese labour did not go down well. Rival gangs had set fire to the Chinese harvesters' cockles. To avoid clashes, the Chinese preferred to go out on the sands after dark.

Identification prospects didn't improve much when, Gordon Copley, a forensic odontologist examined all of the victims, photographing and x-raying teeth, recording dental abnormalities and dental work. It soon emerged that the victims had almost no dental work or decay. The victims' healthy, relatively sugar-free diet meant their teeth would yield little information unless we could match them to family photos of them smiling. Finding the families and talking to them was not going to be easy. Just 46 calls were made to Morecambe's Casualty Bureau, and most of these came from journalists. This was the beginning of the most difficult part of this particular operation, the success of which depended on Family Liaison Officers (FLOs) who collect Ante

Mortem data. I am full of admiration for the people who undertake this most sensitive work. In this case more than ever, the FLOs needed an accurate remit to not only be effective but to keep the distress felt by the families, if and when we found them, to a minimum.

Guidelines vary depending on the type of disaster and the condition of victims. Badly burned bodies for example, will have no fingerprints, so no need to spend precious time at the family home lifting ante-mortem fingerprints.

Apart from fingerprints, the primary means of identification collected by FLOs include DNA, dental charts, and details of unique medical conditions. Teeth, a robust identifier, can survive most accidents and still prove useful after fire and decomposition, when DNA collection, the discovery of a Unique Medical Condition (UMC) and the recovery of fingerprints may be impossible. Permission to access dental records will be gained from the family who have to sign consent forms, and the discovery of gum shields at the family home may also prove useful in terms of indicating a UMC or providing a possible DNA profile.

The key for FLOs is to remain flexible and to think like detectives. Odontologists often request photographs of the deceased. If they discover a recent photograph of the missing person and they are smiling, then it's likely they can be matched by the position and structure of the teeth.

Medical records may reveal UMCs, a history of surgical interventions, sources of DNA or x-rays. The person may have been a blood donor or on the bone marrow donor register and if so, more invaluable and unique data may be available. The frontal sinuses of the face are considered unique, so if X-rays and CT or MRI scans are found in medical records, they should be taken. Allergies and dietary requirements can also be useful identifiers.

Of course, care must be taken with regard to UMCs as it is always possible that more than one person at the same disaster has the same (even rare) condition. Implants (hip replacements for example) sometimes have a serial number stamped into them and this can be linked to an individual.

Tattoos and their placement may also be unique and so these are always recorded, described and photographed and can be matched to family photographs.

Although DNA is an extremely useful and popular tool, it isn't always the best method of identification. Depending on the type of accident, there may be commingling of fluids and body parts and problems of cross-contamination are extremely likely (and this applies to the collection of both ante-mortem and post-mortem data). DNA testing is also expensive and relatively slow, although it is useful when significant fragmentation has taken place, as it will reunite remains. Forensic advisers are always on hand to advise the FLOs on which ante-mortem to collect.

Reference DNA might be on the United Kingdom National DNA Database (NDNAD; officially the UK National Criminal Intelligence DNA Database). Set up in 1995 it holds at the last count the details of just over six million people and is growing by about 30,000 samples each month. It comes from samples recovered from crime scenes, police suspects and, in England and Wales, anyone arrested and detained at a police station.

As DNA is inherited, NDNAD can also be used to indirectly identify many others in the population related to a database subject. It's not perfect and some samples will degrade and become useless (any taken with dry brushes and swabs, for example). In the event of a mass disaster, section 918 of the Serious and Organised Crime Act 2005 allows for the use of DNA from the NDNAD for the purposes of identification.

If reference DNA cannot be traced there are a number of other options to follow. First a DNA profile can be developed using familial DNA. If a DNA profile which is extrapolated from DNA profiles of family members is to be used to established identity, the FLO will have to prepare a comprehensive lineage chart or family tree so that the best advice is taken as to the person from whom the FLO should gather a DNA swab. At all times the FLO needs to keep the family aware of the processes involved and avoid raising expectations regarding timescale in terms of resolving identity.

It is also possible to explore items that the individual is believed to have used and on which they may therefore have left their DNA. Care must be taken in these situations as it is possible that others may have used the items. The following items may be gathered from the home, place of work, inside a motor vehicle, etc.: clothing (preferably unwashed), toothbrush, used cups or mugs, letters or envelopes that the missing person has sealed, a telephone, especially one used exclusively by the missing person, skin cells trapped inside the links of a watch.

The use of fingerprints is limited by the condition of the remains. The collection of fingerprints will follow a similar process to the DNA capture, and knowing the lifestyle and routine of the missing person is highly significant to success. It may be necessary to ask families to hand over valuable and precious items for forensic examination. It is important, as with DNA, that wherever possible fingerprints are taken from something that was handled only by the missing person (fingerprints of family members can be taken for the purposes of exclusion). Fingerprints will always be taken by a specialist as multiple techniques requiring significant levels of skill are required to lift them. It's always a good idea for the FLO to tell the family not to tidy or dust their home (a common response when a loved one is missing as doing something positive, such as readying the home for their return, fills the time) until the fingerprint officer has had a chance to examine the area.

Clothing and items found on the body have to be treated with caution. Items could have been found by someone shortly before the accident and clothing is rarely unique although it can help to find as much information as possible about what someone was wearing, as well as where it was purchased, size, whether there are any familiar stains, rips, replacement buttons, etc. Jewellery might be made unique by inscriptions of names and dates.

Survivor interviews were not helpful. They knew almost nothing (or claimed to know nothing) about one another. The workers called each other by nicknames. Some survivors ran away from the temporary accommodation they were placed in. Before they'd run off however, interpreters had managed to establish that they spoke Mandarin with a Fujianese dialect and were therefore from Fujian Province.

One survivor did explain how they were overcome. Li Hua was in the cocklers' vehicle when the sea started to lift it from the ground. He described how people, panicking, jumped out of the vehicle and tried to swim , how they were immediately overcome by the fast currents and were dragged below the water's surface. Li Hua tried to swim and found himself alone. He had all-but given up and was waiting to die when he was spotted by a search and rescue helicopter.

Fishing permits we recovered were in false names. Addresses were searched and prints were recovered, but evidence remained scant.

The Immigration Service proved to be extremely useful, however. Many of the victims had been arrested trying to enter the country by immigration officers, or had sought political asylum. This led to nine photographs, linked by the victims' fingerprint identification, being sent to the Chinese police. A further four victims were found through the police's databases. Meanwhile, the national DNA database resulted in two matches of ante-mortem and post-mortem profiles for males 11 and 14 (each victim was numbered, with the prefix M or F for Male or

Female). When we had done all we could with the bodies, at least for the moment, the Coroner ordered them placed in deep freeze (wherever you die and whoever you are, the Coroner decides everything to do with what happens to your body, from analysis to storage and release) and Steve Brunksill and his team reached out to the Chinese.

China was by this time reacting to the incident with understandable outrage. What had been allowed to happen to their citizens was inexcusable. One newspaper headline screamed *The Devil's Beach!* The Chinese were understandably angry not only at the deaths but at how terribly the victims had been treated before they died. The FLO officers would have to tread extremely delicately. I put Steve in touch with a retired police officer, a friend and colleague of mine, Detective Superintendent Dennis McGookin, who in Kent in June 2000 had ended up trying to identify a group of 58 dead Chinese people from Fujian province who had suffocated in a shipping container on one of the hottest days of the year. I knew he had given presentations on how he had identified the victims and he was able to provide us with invaluable information in terms of working with the Chinese authorities. The victims in this incident, also smuggled to the UK by snakehead gangs, were also from the province of Fujian and Dennis was only able to provisionally identify four of the victims until he travelled to China.

In all, eighteen officers were involved with the identification enquiries at Morecambe and the key players, it turned out, were two Chinese-speaking officers: PC Kwok Chee Cheung from Greater Manchester Police who joined the operation on February 6 and Superintendent Matthew Kwok from Interpol, who was based in Lyon, France, and had some experience of snakehead gangs. Between them, their specialist knowledge, not to mention translation skills (PC Cheung translated tonnes of Chinese documents that were seized during the operation), saved the day.

Also invaluable was DNA expert Zuo Zhijin, who'd served two years with Interpol in Lyon specialising in disaster victim identification. He led a team of five officers who visited the families of the victims that we'd provisionally identified. PC Cheung accompanied officers on two trips to China, the first of which was all about establishing the identity of the victims.

Once the Chinese had all our information, the Chinese police were able to provisionally identify 18 of the 20 victims recovered at this time. By the time a UK identification team travelled to China in April we were fairly certain we had all 23 victims' families correctly identified. One complicating factor was that some people didn't want to talk out of fear of the snakehead gangs. But with the help of Chinese police, the officers duly performed their family liaison role, collecting ante-mortem data and showing personal items of property and post-mortem photographs of the deceased to their nearest relatives. If the personal items were identified then they were returned to the family. Final results of DNA tests were received from the forensic science service within two weeks of the team's return to the UK and identification process was complete and the victims were repatriated from the Coroner's deep freeze units in Lancashire to China.

There was one, entirely accidental blunder, however. It used to be that we would tie a label with the victim identification number around a wrist, if available and the matching number would be written on the body bag's label. I noticed that sometimes, especially during the lifting and shifting part of an operation, that the labels tore or snapped. So, after Selby, I ordered hundreds of hospital tags. These are made of tough plastic and are fixed by a press-stud and once pressed, the only way to get it off is to cut it. For body parts several tags can be connected together to circle it. I ordered some in for Lancashire, and they were red with a white background. The only piece of negative feedback we got from the whole operation was that we shouldn't use red. Red is sign of joy in China and some distraught relatives saw this as insult. We only use white tags now.

The Morecambe Bay tragedy led to a huge and complex police operation and although it seemed for a while as though the people responsible would escape justice, gangmasters Lin Liang Ren, Zhao Xiao Qing and Lin Mu Yong were arrested on suspicion of manslaughter and facilitation (facilitation is a criminal offence of enabling illegal immigrants to work in this country). With the help of survivor Li Hua, who now lives in the UK under the witness protection programme, they were subsequently successfully prosecuted and Operation Lund (as the case was called) won that year's top criminal justice award.

The man in charge, Lin Liang Ren, who gambled £600 on a single hand of blackjack at a casino the night before he sent 23 people to their deaths, was convicted of 21 counts of manslaughter as well as facilitating illegal immigration and perverting the course of justice. In the face of competition from other Chinese teams along the Bay, Ren cut out the local buyers and controlled the production, selling directly to outlets himself. To avoid fights with rival gangs, he sent his cocklers out against the advice of tidal charts and safety rules (all anyone else seemed to care about was the bottom line).

Ren was jailed for 14 years in March 2006 but was released after just eight and returned to China, where his wealthy family have several homes. Ren, a gambling-mad former accountant who drove a sports car and lived in a smart home while his workers slept ten to a room in squalor, had never showed remorse. He served less than four months for each life lost.

Despite Ren's early release, I like to think that the men and women who died did not do so entirely in vain. The events in Morecambe led to *The Gangmasters Licensing Act* 2004, designed to end the exploitation of immigrant workers.

As I said, I'd like to think that, but sadly, exploitation continues apace.

One local fisherman said: "In the summer of 2003, I rescued fifty to sixty Chinese folk who were stranded while cockling for a gangmaster... That should have been a warning." We missed our chance then. But even as late as October 2011, 17 cockle pickers of eastern European origin were saved at the River Ribble estuary in Lancashire, just thirty miles from the Morecambe Bay disaster. These workers had no knowledge of the sea and hadn't been given any safety equipment or guidance by their gang master.

On hearing the news, Mr Hua said he still has panic attacks almost a decade after the tragedy. Speaking to the BBC, he said: "I think a lot about those who didn't survive, particularly at Chinese New Year, because it happened around that time... We all came for the same reason. We left our families to make a better life. And they were gone just like that. I was just lucky."

And as Mick Gradwell, now retired from Lancashire Police, said: "You're thrown into investigating international organised crime gangs, snakeheads, triads, international human trafficking... We dealt with the people who were responsible for the deaths on the night... But we did not make any dent into these wider criminal gangs who traffic people around the world... The main reason 23 people died in Morecambe Bay on this particular night was because of poverty in the Fujian province of China."

The FLOs who travelled 5,000 miles to Fujian province not only saw the grieving families, they saw people left in conditions unthinkable in the UK where, after a tragedy like this, people would be entitled to compensation and would receive every support our society is able to offer. In Fujian, no one received compensation, only a near-insignificant amount of charity at best, and to this day they have to fend off debt collectors so aggressive that they drive the families to new depths of despair.

China, a society which has recently discovered a love of free enterprise and the wealth it can bring, lacks a social welfare system, meaning that those at the bottom live on a knife-edge. Travelling abroad to seek one's fortune is seen as a way out of what seems an otherwise impossible situation. Fujianese people have searched for wealth abroad for more than a century and the snakeheads tap into this tradition, which is today driven by economic hardship. The snakeheads feed hopeful young people the idea that there's easy money to be made abroad. It seems like an attractive option when the alternative is to join tens of millions of peasants who labour in Chinese factories making products for westerners.

The FLOs heard Fujian mourning as they visited the families. This is a hypnotic and desolate melodic cry, a song that mourns not only the loss of the loved one but the devastation their death leaves behind.

The victims and their families had been charged up to £20,000 by the snakehead gangs. As most families in Fujian Province earn less than £1,000 a year, a deposit would be paid, the rest being paid out of the immigrants' earnings, working for the snakeheads, once in the UK, who would also provide accommodation (a necessary means of controlling their slaves).

When someone says they're going abroad, people almost rush to lend them money for the trip and to pay the snakeheads because it's seen as a good investment, and will be more than repaid in a couple of years or so. But when it goes wrong there's no safety net. According to tradition, the spouse and children inherit the debts of the deceased father or mother (and end up paying ten per cent interest). The most help a family in dire straits can hope for from the government is £3 per month per child.

Although many fail to get to Europe and find work, some do succeed, and it is possible to see the effect of European earnings made by illegal immigrants in the construction and improvements of family houses – all paid for by money sent from abroad. This is all the encouragement thousands of young hopefuls need. And it is this that drives more young people into the arms of the snakeheads – as well as the fact that the poor of Fujian see China's growing economic strength and they want to be a part of it, to own a piece of it, and the fastest way, the only way for a young factory worker, is to head overseas.

It is hard to imagine the psychological effects on the team by seeing so many grieving families in such a short space of time, and then to see the life they'd been left with, which to us in the UK seems like no life worth living at all.

Cao Chaokun left behind his wife Zhou Xiaomei and son Cao Xianyong 13, daughter Cao Meiyun 16 with debts of 200,000 yuan (£13,250) and a monthly income 250 yuan (£17). Zhou Xiaomei lives in a tiny cottage surrounded by new-build, European-style monstrosities of homes and apartments that seem to have grown up around her almost overnight. Cao was on his way to getting an education in the UK when he died on Morecambe sands. Now Zhou mixes concrete for a living and her children, stick thin, survive on noodles, rice and the odd, tiny piece of meat. Zhou also looks after Cao's brother who is nearly paralysed, and who can't afford the operation and treatment that would cure him.

Guo Binlong left behind his wife Yu Lihong, daughter Guo Yuwei 13, son Guo Minghui 6 with debts of 300,000 yuan (£20,000) and with an income of 750 yuan (£50) per month. Guo called home from Morecambe Bay, shortly before he drowned. His mother took the call. He said the water was up to his neck and that they should pray for him.

We now know, thanks to the work of journalist Jonathan Watts who went to China for the Guardian newspaper to interview some of the victims' families three years after the disaster that a year after Guo's death, unable to stand the constant harassment of the creditors who demanded £20,000 in repayments (the original loan was £5,300), Guo's mother drank rat poison. Guo's youngest son found her body. At first he thought she was sleeping. They hadn't paid back any of the money they owed and were on the run from creditors. The children face a future of working to pay off the debts of their father, who decided to try his luck in the UK after his brick-making business collapsed.

Wu Hongkang left a wife, Su Zhenqin and two daughters aged seven and eleven. His family inherited a debt of 300,000 yuan (£19,900) and the family's monthly income was 300 yuan (£20). Her prized possession was her wedding album, she in white dress, Wu in a suit. A smiling portrait of the two of them with their two children was taken a few days before he left for Europe with hope in his heart. Her husband's death meant instant ruin. Su mixed concrete to earn a 'living' of £20 but couldn't afford to heat or repair her crumbling home, let alone repay her debts.

Dong Xinwu left behind his wife Chen Yanchun, son Song Xinyao, 14, and two grandmothers with a debt of 240,000 yuan (£15,900). Their monthly income of 500 yuan (£33), earned by Chen who hammered shoe soles, left them with no way of paying it back. Chen sold her jewellery but still had no hope of repaying friends and family, let alone the Snakeheads, who leant Dong the money to get to Europe so he could make enough to send his son to university, a truly impossible dream as they couldn't even afford to keep him in high school. Song planned to apply for a job at MacDonalds (the salary is about £33 per month) so he could start paying off the family debts as soon as possible.

Lin Guoguang left behind his wife Chen Jinyun and sons Lin Luan, 16, and Lin Huan, 15 with debts of 100,000 yuan (£6,625). Their monthly income 600 yuan (£40), was earned from cleaning houses. It was only enough to pay 50% of the monthly interest their debts incurred. Lin wrote to his wife saying that his life in Europe was like being in jail, that he would never make his fortune. As if with some awful foreknowledge, he signed off his last letter with fatherly advice, telling his sons to study hard and never act proud and to always listen to their mother. Lin Luan and Lin Huan's dreams of university will remain just that.

Chen Aiqin left behind her son Cai Zhixiang, 13, daughter Cai Huiling, ten, with debts of 150,000 yuan (£9,940) and a monthly income of 2,000 yuan (£132). Their father died years earlier, an event that drove the family into debt. Chen thought going to Europe was the only way out of this hole. The debt was inherited by Chen's brother who, after three years, had managed to chip away only a small portion. Jonathan Watts reported that Cai wanted to stop studying and find work to start paying off the snakeheads.

Xu Yuhua and Liu Qinying left behind their son, Xu Bin, 14 with debts of 200,000 yuan (£13,250) and a monthly income of 1,200 yuan (£80). Xu Bin's debts were taken over by his father's sister, Aunt Xu Liying, whose salary would have been adequate for most families but, thanks to the number of dependents and the size of the family debt, she now lives in poverty. Xu Liying has a photograph of Xu Yuhua and Liu Qinying smiling on Morecambe Beach. Her brother went to the UK to earn money to pay for their mother's cancer treatment and his wife was persuaded to follow after the snakeheads warned her that migrant men go off with other women if they are away for long periods. The creditors have turned the dead couple's house into a storeroom. Their orphan son spends his school holidays working in a factory for 60p a day to start repaying the family debts, knowing the creditors will come after him the moment he turns eighteen. Xu Bin wrote to the judge in the Morecambe Bay trial: "The accident was a disaster for me. I had a warm and happy family even though we weren't rich. Now I have lost my parents. My uncle, auntie and grandfather help me. But I have a few hundred thousand yuan worth of debts. Although they don't say anything, I know they worry every day about debt."

Lin Zhifang left behind his father Lin Guohua with debts of 100,000 yuan (£6,625) and no income. Lin Zhifang was, at 18-years-old, the youngest victim of the Morecambe Bay tragedy. He had left school early to work in a factory but did not want to accept that poverty was his lot in life and decided to take his chances in the UK. Also, he reasoned, he would never find a bride unless he was able to earn enough to buy his own home. Within eight weeks he was dead. Lin Guohua is a farmer without land – they moved from the remote countryside to be nearer to a city school- and too old to find work in a factory. He survives on handouts from relatives and tells the creditors that threaten him with beatings that he can't repay and begs for time. The interest increases the debt by £66 each month.

The victims' families want justice and compensation and talked of human rights. They are angry. They have been left alone with impossible burdens. They condemn the gangs who tricked their loved ones – the chief breadwinners of the family – to travel to the other side of the world in search of a new and better life, a life that would benefit their entire families. All lies. Many feel as though we in Britain treated their relatives like criminals and feel outrage towards their own government who has done nothing to help them. No one wants to take responsibility. And those who were found guilty of the crimes of manslaughter seem to be better treated than the victims' families. While the chief gang master was freed after just eight years in prison and returned to China where he has a wealthy family waiting to take care of him, the relatives of the cockle pickers look ahead and see a life of poverty and depression stretching ahead until their own deaths.

That doesn't feel like justice to me.

ELEVEN

A MILLION TINY PIECES

At the time, I barely had time to register the experiences of Morecambe. Just days after finishing the initial examinations, I completed a pre-booked training course in Humberside and finished with my traditional, politely-delivered message that I hoped they'd never see me again, "professionally anyway."

The next day I got a call from Humberside police.

"There's been a little incident and we need your expertise."

The caller was Detective Superintendent Rich Kerman. Rich had been on another one of my courses the previous year. When he said 'little', what he meant was that it wasn't a major disaster that would make the national news but that there were issues over victim identification for what would turn out to be a benchmark-setting case.

A Cessna 310 (a twin-engine monoplane with a capacity of six) had crashed twenty minutes after take off, at around 1pm on March 13, 2004, close to the village of Hotham, a few miles west of Hull. Two passengers were on board, a student and his trainer. They were listed on the passenger manifest and the control tower had seen them off. The recovery teams were able to find fingerprints from body parts recovered at the scene, which they were confident would help establish the identity the two people on the manifest and DNA tests would satisfy the Coroner as to who was on the plane.

"So what's the problem?" I asked.

"The number of body parts."

Twenty-five officers from the Victim Recovery Team had found over 2,000 parts for two deceased. The question was: Do you have to ID every body part to make sure the right bits go to the right family? Although the natural immediate instinct is to say yes, the problem was the size of the body parts. Most of them were tiny. And the scene had not been handled well. If I'd known, I would have engaged the help of forensic anthropologists who – thanks to some remarkable skills and extremely specialised knowledge – understand the mapping and recovery of human remains and today play a vital role in many cases of DVI. I suspected – depending on the route we would choose to take with this case – that we would need the help of a forensic anthropologist in the mortuary.

Forensic anthropology involves the application of scientific techniques to assist with the identification of human remains, whether intact, fragmented, burned or skeletonised. They attempt to establish four major biological identifiers: sex, age, height and ancestral origin (race). At disaster sites they will help to determine of the minimum number of individuals present (MNI), the separation of human from nonhuman remains and will interpret pathologies, trauma and surgical interventions to reconstruct a person, also using ante-mortem data such as x-rays or photographs of the deceased that show body modifications (tattoos or body piercings, for example). They can also help with facial identification through superimposition and reconstruction.

Forensic anthropologists are these days in high demand to identify the living in cases of human trafficking and immigration, using methods such as vein pattern recognition analysis and facial recognition from CCTV footage. Despite the ever-increasing demand for their services, there are few full-time forensic anthropologists and most are employed in universities as lecturers. All are members of the Centre for International Forensics Assistance (CIFA) and their professional association is the British Association of Human Identification (BAHID).

In a disaster scenario like the one at Hotham, forensic anthropologists are invaluable to investigators, recovery and identification teams. They can spot evidence of commingling, identify body parts and fragments, and advise on how best to retrieve body parts. It's easy to miss small body parts when searching a disaster site, even when the incident is small like Hotham, debris can be cast over a wide area and can end up being obscured by crops and undergrowth.

Even then, it is not always immediately obvious even to the trained eye what is human and what is not. Sheep had been grazing in the vicinity of the crash site and it would not have been immediately obvious after such extreme fragmentation which bone pieces were human and which came from sheep (or other field animals). In other incidents, where bomb blasts have taken place in restaurants for example, the recovery and identification teams are hampered by the bones of pigs, chickens, cows, sheep, fish, deer and even more exotic animals. Similarly, as with the London underground terrorist attacks of July 7 2005, bombs detonated on busy transport systems may result in the presence of non-human remains, from pets travelling on the train, animal products in passengers' shopping, as well as vermin and other environment-specific species. In other environments, small horse bones can easily be mistaken for human fingers; the ribs of a pig are similar to human ribs, and the bones within the flipper of a seal can be confused with the human hand. A forensic anthropologist has to be ready for the unexpected as non-native species can turn up in unusual places (reptiles such as snakes and lizards are relatively common pets, for example). For this reason, the forensic anthropologist needs to be confident not only in the identification of human remains but those of all vertebrate species.

Identification problems can also come from other kinds of commingling. After Hurricane Katrina the bones of the long-dead were recovered alongside those of the recently deceased after cemeteries were washed away. The chief difficulty for victim identification after the 9/11 attacks was that it was left to firefighters, inexperienced in victim recovery and without professional levels of anatomical knowledge, to collect the fragmented remains of people, so there was a great deal of commingling as a result.

The discipline of forensic anthropology relies more on experience than technical instruments. The adult human skeleton has approximately 206 bones and the forensic anthropologist has to be able to identify all of them – whether whole or in pieces. Some bones are better than others for establishing identity and some tend to be tougher and are more likely to survive than others but the forensic anthropologist has no control over which parts of the body will be recovered, not to mention what condition they might be in, so the task demands total proficiency in bone analysis.

Forensic anthropologists rely chiefly on calipers, an osteometric board (a bone ruler) and their extensive specialist knowledge. Sometimes they will use a microwave to remove small pieces of flesh from bones (a process known as maceration) so the bones can be properly measured and examined. This is time-consuming, noxious and to be avoided as a general rule, only used if identification is proving especially difficult. Dermested beetle colonies (long-used by taxidermists to clean bones) are sometimes used for delicate specimens but this takes far too long for most circumstances.

Sex, age and height can all be determined from bone measurements, whether the bones are whole or fragmented. Forensic anthropologists look at growth plates to establish age and employ mathematical regression formulae to calculate height from the length of long bones.

As for telling what part of the body a small piece recovered from an accident site might belong to, a cross-section will show the skin and hair (which can be determined as being axillary, pubic or limb hair) muscles, bones, fat, blood vessels and nerves. The form of the bone would indicate which part of the limb is represented such as single bone in the upper arm and thigh, two bones side-by-side in the forearm and lower leg. Muscle groups will also show whether this is the upper or lower part of that limb. The position of nerves and blood vessels go some way to determine whether it is the right or the left limb.

If the pelvis is available then this will allow for the determination of the person's sex as the male and female pelvis bones are distinct, the female pelvis being distinct by virtue of the birth canal. Male skeletons are heavier than females and the greater muscle mass of males means that they show more pronounced sites of attachment to the bone, and results in bones that are stronger and larger. The supra-orbital region of the skull (the area above the eyes) also tends to be more rugged in males, often exhibiting marked brow ridges.

It was a pity that we hadn't been able to get a forensic anthropologist to the crash site as getting it right on-site allows for faster identification in the mortuary. An obvious solution in this case would seem to be DNA. Testing speed and accuracy had improved enormously by 2004, thanks to pioneering work by the International Commission on Missing Persons (ICMP) which was set up to investigate missing persons cases in the Balkans; "people killed or had gone missing as a result of wars, ethnic conflicts, human rights abuses, and humanitarian and natural disasters." The ICMP was a unique and incredible institution born from the unthinkable horror of a genocidal war.

Up to 30,000 people were listed as missing after the war that took place in the former Yugoslavia from 1992–1995. Most of the victims were the end result of ethnic cleansing operations that featured concentration camps and mass killings. The war forced one million people from their homes, left 30,000 missing and 100,000 confirmed dead.

A huge section of the surviving population was afflicted by trauma-related illnesses. They needed closure, they needed to know where their loved ones were so that they could start coming to terms with what had happened, to start thinking about the future.

The most famous case dealt with by the ICMP was the Srebrenica massacre. On July 13 1995, soldiers rounded up about 6,000 emaciated Bosnian Muslims outside the small spa town of Srebrenica in eastern Bosnia and Herzegovina and took them, many barefooted and stripped to the waist, to a football field. General Ratko Mladić visited the men twice and told them they would be treated as prisoners of war, and would be swapped for Bosnian Serbs being held captive by the army of Bosnia and Herzegovina. Instead, 1,500 of the men were taken to agricultural warehouses; a similar number were taken to a school; 1,100 to a farm; 400 to a factory; 500 to a cultural centre and somewhere between 1,500 and 2,000 to a dam and another school. Between the afternoon of July 14 and the evening of July 16, they were machine-gunned. As new prisoners arrived at each shooting site, in groups of five to ten men, hands bound, they saw bodies covering the ground. Then they were lined up and shot. This was the largest mass murder in Europe since World War II.

As the war drew to an end and it became obvious that war crimes were going to be investigated, the Bosnian Serbs attempted to hide the evidence by digging up the remains and moving them to dozens of sites – woods, valleys, farmyards, in fields near minor roads – up to twenty miles from Srebrenica, over some 300 mi.^{2} of countryside that featured pine forests, mountains, ravines and gorges. This lead not only to commingling but meant that remains of some individuals, broken up by bulldozers and mechanical diggers ended up at four different sites.

The Srebrenica massacre of 1995 provided the ICMP's DNA laboratory system with what one scientist called "the world's greatest forensic puzzle." Approximately 8,100 people were reported missing after the fall of Srebrenica. With 206 bones in a human adult skeleton, that meant there were 1,668,000 bones to be found, dug up, sorted and identified.

An international team of archaeologists and forensic anthropologists performed the recovery of human remains. Self-winding watches, still on victims' wrists confirmed the time and date of the executions. The position of bodies was mapped using twelve anatomical landmarks, the placement of the skull, wrists, elbows, shoulders and other body parts, and the data entered into archaeological software that allowed 3-D images to be rotated 360°. This allowed the investigators to learn how the bodies were placed and with what – and who might have been there doing it.

From 1996 to 1999, the team filled 6,353 body bags. The smell meant they had to be stored in local salt mines but when the rats moved in it was decided to build the world's first super mortuary, a building large enough to hold different remains of hundreds of bodies. It was constructed in the parking lot of a funeral home in Tuzla – Bosnia's economic, scientific and cultural centre.

The ICMP's new DNA identification technique was key to its success. Small blood samples were taken from thousands of relatives; drops were placed upon a small card sealed in airtight polythene bags. Sections of victims' bones were ground up and DNA was extracted from them and computers searched for matches.

RICHARD VENABLES

Usually, one highly-qualified DNA analyst would perform each step of the process of identification. This is what makes it slow and extremely expensive. In Bosnia, the ICMP decided to use an assembly-line with different technicians completing each stage of the analysis. They also had access to employees who could be paid a lot less than what they'd earn elsewhere in Europe in 2000. Unemployment was off-the-scale in Bosnia and there were plenty of young and overqualified scientists ready to work for a few hundred pounds a month. It also helped to have Bosnian staff as the process involved substantial interaction with local people who were naturally suspicious of foreign teams sent in to do such a sensitive job.

Their first identification came in November 2001, using DNA, of the remains of a fifteen-year-old boy from Srebrenica. Another 518 identifications followed over the next twelve months. Gradually, over the coming years, hundreds and then thousands of identified bodies were buried, given the funerals their relatives desperately wanted. By 2010 the ICMP had collected a staggering 69,922 blood samples from relatives of victims for Bosnia alone and analysed 28,826 bone samples. By the end of July 2010 the ICMP had made a total of 13,135 identifications of persons missing from Bosnia and Herzegovina during the war – Srebrenica included – based upon the number of the successful DNA matches. Only a small fraction of the 6,481 known victims of the Srebrenica Massacre had been identified by the ICMP at this stage, however. But their desperately important work continues. They are identifying people exterminated because they belonged to the "wrong" nationality, religion, race, class, gender, or political group. Their work proved that these people existed and these atrocities happened, making sure there could be no chance of denial. In the words of the International Herald Tribune the ICMP was using DNA technology to "map a human genocide". And the laboratory system proved to be so precise that it was considered good enough to be used in evidence in war crimes trials in The Hague, which continue to this day. Countries from Iraq to Colombia have since requested the assistance of the ICMP.

Unfortunately for us in Yorkshire in 2004, DNA remained prohibitively expensive and the ICMP was too busy with its own investigations to help us and the costs and practicalities of sending body parts abroad to be analysed at the ICMP's labs would have been just as prohibitive.

The cost in the UK of DNA testing was at that time £400 per analysis per part, and this would have more than wiped out the Coroner's budget for the year ; the Coroner – at this time Geoff Saul, an extremely experienced and practical man who had not encountered an issue like this before – had an annual budget of around £750,000, so even if he'd of used it all, he'd still be at least £100,000 short. The police only pay for DNA testing in relation to criminal investigations.

It also took up to 72 hours to complete each test and there were only so many testers and therefore samples that could be processed in any one day. When I spoke to a forensic specialist he told me it would take the best part of a year to work through all of the remains. Part of the reason for this would be that more urgent and active criminal investigations would take priority, i.e., cases of rape and murder, each one of which could generate dozens of tests.

Hotham provided us with a unique situation. More than 170 body parts had been recovered at Dunkeswick and we were able to rely on best mechanical fit with the pathologist always having the final say and with no DNA tests necessary. At the Selby rail crash it was possible, even for the non-medically trained, to match limbs to bodies, using clues such as the same shirt, same skin and so on, although we also double-checked using DNA (there being far fewer parts), so we could be one hundred per cent certain that all were accurately returned to their loved ones.

In total we had 2,048 body parts at Hotham. The pathologist explained as he examined the pieces how in some cases parts had been forced into one another, i.e., bone had been blasted out of one body and , possibly, into the muscle of the other. I took some time to study the parts that were arrayed before me. It occurred to me that I was going to have to draw a line somewhere as to what is a "body part". Most of the smaller pieces were under 10cm long, so, after discussing this with the Coroner and the SIM, we agreed that this would be our benchmark. Anything under 10cm long would be classified as Human Residual Tissue and disposed of respectfully.

We worked our way through every piece, the pathologist confirming whether each piece we selected, after measuring it, was large enough to be a body part or not. I stopped short when I came to a small piece that did not fit into this new identification criteria: four teeth still attached to the gums. Clearly this was human, but did we have the right to reject this as being part of the remains to be DNA'd and returned? Clearly, some body parts less than 10cm in length could still be anatomically identified by the pathologist, so we amended the policy to include anything that was less then 10cm and recognisable as being a specific part of human anatomy.

By the time we'd finished 1,998 pieces were Human Residual Tissue. The body parts that had met the criteria for identification were re-bagged, re-labelled and sent for DNA testing. When these were returned to us, we were certain that body parts had been correctly identified and could be returned to the families for burial.

At this point, Rich took me to one side. "This term, Human Residual Tissue, I'm afraid that this TLA (Three Letter Acronym) has already been taken."

I thought for a moment and then turned red with embarrassment. Hormone Replacement Therapy! We decided a better name would be RHT: Residual Human Tissue.

I always believe in full disclosure to the families of victims who, in my experience, understand the difficulties of our work in a manner so graceful to be inspirational. Body recovery and identification is not something they should have to worry about but major disasters sometimes force the issue. In this case, Geoff Saul, along with Rich Kerman, visited the families and provided them with full and accurate info about the condition of their loved ones' remains, and that we had to draw a line somewhere in terms of recovery and identification. He assured them that the parts they would return had most definitely been correctly identified and that the rest, although human, could not be assigned to an individual. They accepted this with tremendous grace and the Coroner paid for a third funeral, a cremation for the RHT.

The cause of the accident was never established. Experts told the inquest that there seemed to be nothing wrong with the plane and it was not known which pilot was in control at the time, and so the inquest jury returned verdicts of accidental death for both men.

This benchmark was adjusted in the aftermath of the July 7, 2005 bombings in London, where 52 people were killed and 700 injured by suicide bombers. It was decided that as my measurement only dealt with length and it would be better to work to volume, so the parameters for RHT were re-defined as 5cm cubed.

As part of my full time role I was now a member of the government's Mass Fatalities Group, which contained representatives from many agencies involved in disaster response. It was at one such meeting that I became aware of the charity called Disaster Action. I was, as ever, obsessively keen to improve the way we worked and decided to get in touch. As it turned out, it was clear I still had some way to go in terms of knowledge and improvement.

Disaster Action is an umbrella charity, formed in 1991 by people who had lost relatives and/or friends in each major disaster of the 1980s, and who had already formed support groups for each one of these disasters: Lockerbie, Hillsborough, Marchioness, Herald of Free Enterprise, Kegworth air disaster, Kings Cross fire, Bradford City Stadium fire, Manchester Airport runway fire, etc. Membership is open to anyone who has been involved in the disaster in the UK, or is from the UK and has been affected by disaster anywhere in the world.

Pam Dix, one of the founders of Disaster Action, described how support groups helped victims' relatives and survivors deal with the inescapable emotions of shock, grief and anger, emotions that normally have a destructive effect on people. By channeling these emotions into a support group, people are able to focus on building something positive out of the disaster. Being part of a support group also allows people to share their experience and, having suffered similarly, they quickly form strong bonds, and feel they can talk about their experience without fear of judgement.

Unlike friends, who share your pain but want you to feel better and believe there comes a point where you should be better and start to live beyond it, people who have lived through disaster understand how your life has been changed forever, and that it's impossible to ever get back to 'normal'. This common grief frees people from the need to explain their pain so that they will understand; fellow sufferers understand immediately and this allows them to move forward together in positive ways without ever having to put the past behind them.

I knew exactly what they meant about the common bond disaster creates. It also affects rescue workers and people like myself who are involved in the recovery operation. A decade after Dunkeswick I was in a pub in Bridlington when a man I recognized from the temporary mortuary walked in. We hadn't seen each other since the disaster, the only time we'd ever met but, at this chance encounter, it was like we were long-lost friends. We embraced and I felt an incredible urge to reconcile with him. We talked about Dunkeswick for a while, shook hands and we went our separate ways. I haven't seen him since but I know that if we were to bump into one another again, or if I were to see any of that team, our reactions would be the same.

The driving principles behind Disaster Action, whose members all came from vastly different backgrounds, with different religious beliefs, was not only about supporting one another, it was a group that asked questions about how and why people had died and been injured and how similar disasters might be prevented in the future.

To quote from their manifesto:

"As we go about our daily life we never stop to think that we are actually putting it in the hands of others.

We assume planes are airworthy.

We take it for granted the rail signalling equipment is properly maintained.

We expect staff to be trained in live evacuation procedures.

We can't imagine how profit motives could come before public safety.

Disaster action is a charity formed by a group of people who thought that way too. Until we felt the pain of losing loved ones, in disasters.

Our committee is made up of individuals and representatives from all the family groups set up after recent tragedies.

As an umbrella group for these grassroots organisations, we are well aware of the dreadful common thread running through these disasters.

They weren't acts of God's will.

They'd needn't have happened.

Preventing future disasters is the main aim of Disaster Action.

We don't want anyone else to go through what we've been through."

I'd seen how the media and politicians had on occasion treated probing questions about families who had lost loved ones in disasters as though they were motivated by revenge, born from an inability to move on, when this was clearly not the case. By joining forces, they have a clearer voice which is taken more seriously by government and media, and which come to rely upon the group for information, to help the government make the right decision about such things as memorials, or the scope of an inquiry, or even things as basic as where an inquiry should be held.

Company directors and other senior officials rightly take credit in the good times so too must they acknowledge and accept responsibility when things go tragically wrong.

Pam Dix lost her brother Peter, 35, a management consultant, in the bombing of Pan Am 103 on December 21 1988, which killed 270 people. The families continue to meet to this day, over 25 years on, as a group for mutual support and to discuss the unresolved issues. Civil litigation against Pan Am in the United States eventually lead to the airline being found to be wilfully negligent. The two accused bombers were tried for the murders in a special court in The Hague in 1999. One was cleared, the other convicted and imprisoned in Scotland. Released on "compassionate grounds" because of illness in August 2009, Abdelbaset al-Megrahi was allowed to return to his home country of Libya where he died in 2012. The criminal case remains active to this day.

Pam Dix said of her support group: "Families were only able to meet because one person had been sent a list of contacted shows for the next of kin in the UK anonymously or someone who must have understood how important meeting each other would be. It was an emotional and painful occasion. Mothers, fathers, siblings and partners shared their stories, considering what such a dramatically altered future would now hold, above all wanting answers to the questions of how and why it had happened."

The Marchioness Action Group was formed after the tragedy that took place on the River Thames in London on Sunday August 20 1989. On a warm clear night with a full moon, the brightly lit pleasure boat Marchioness, full of young people enjoying themselves at a party began its trip which ended in disaster when the Bowbelle dredger struck and sank the Marchioness, killing 51 young people.

The Marchioness Action Group had to fight for a full inquest and public enquiry that came over a decade after the disaster. The recommendations in Lord Justice Clark's report into the *Identification of Victims Following a Major Transportation Accident* have had a highly significant impact on the way in which individuals are treated following disasters. Without the commitment of the Marchioness survivors and bereaved, however, the public enquiry would not have taken place and these telling recommendations – which have influenced my work among many others – would not have been made.

After every major disaster in the 1980s, the friends and families of those who died banded together to try and find justice, to make sure that mistakes weren't repeated. Those of us whose lives have been unaffected by disaster owe them a debt of gratitude. They have helped to make our world a much safer place.

As Disaster Action says: "After every disaster a minister or public figure declares gravely this must never happen again. Enquiries may be held, committees may be made. Recommendations are produced, yet still the disasters continue.

Our aim is to break the cycle of tragedy and misery. Once and for all, we intend to learn the lessons of recent disasters and campaign for fundamental changes in the law and in business attitudes.

We believe that these changes will encourage a new corporate culture. One where safety comes first."

They have achieved amazing results in driving forward public inquiries and inquests, not least of which is the Hillsborough Inquest, which began in 2014, more than 25 years after the tragedy.

There is perhaps a perception in some in the fields of justice, the media and among the public that disasters are accidents and that no one is responsible. People have raised this point in recent cases involving death on the roads. For example in the Guardian Newspaper on March 7, 2015 Susannah Rustin wrote: "Could it be that, unlike in trials of people accused of using guns or knives, many of us (juries, judges, police officers, journalists) find it all too easy to imagine being the defendants in such cases? Do we secretly sympathise with the driver who ran a red light, drove too fast or sent a text at the wheel? Is the consequence that we do not feel or think enough about the victims of these crimes?"

There is something similar about disasters because millions of people work on railways, trains, ferries and airlines; in road haulage, in football grounds, sporting arenas, fairs, amusement parks and festivals, and know how easy it is to make a simple mistake, or miss some factor that could end up costing human lives. Just because someone has been killed by a faulty railway signal, it doesn't make it less of a death than someone killed by a knife wound sustained in an assault, or someone who is punched, falls to the ground and dies after cracking their skull on the kerb. For the families and friends of those who have died in disasters, to have to live for the rest of their lives with the knowledge of injustice, or simply without the truth of how their loved one died being publicly established is devastating.

I met with Disaster Action because I knew we could do more in DVI that would help the families of people who had been caught up in disaster. It was something I knew I had to do but at the same time I was nervous about what it would be like, to talk to people who had, in some cases, gone through additional anxiety and trauma inadvertently caused by the emergency services.

Pam and her colleagues were able to voice far better than I ever could what was so important about DVI and would we could do better. Stories from their members who had not had their loved ones found and/or identified confirmed just how important DVI is. For example, as of the 10th anniversary of the 9/11 attacks in New York, 1,124 of the 2,753 people killed remained unidentified, yet efforts continue on the part of the chief medical examiner's office in New York, with thirty names being added to the list of the identified between 2006 and 2011.

In their book *Collective Conviction: The Story of Disaster Action*, Anne Eyre and Pam Dix wrote of 9/11: "[Non-identification] affects all those waiting for the identification of a loved one, whether for a week, a month a year or for ever. The missing are physically absent but psychologically present. There is incredible stress associated with living with this. Normal rituals are not possible. The waiting is incredibly difficult because it messes up the natural processes... It is like living with a chronic illness – eventually we find ways of living with it."

Knowing that the work continues is vital for the families. It's what they deserve at the very least. Often however, especially with regard to earlier disasters, identification will never be made because of decisions made at the time, often without foresight and proper consideration of the families' wishes, such as cremation of unidentified remains.

Disaster Action argue that the use of DNA should be used cautiously, which I am in agreement with. As I've mentioned, it takes time and requires access to specialists and equipment, both of which come at a high price. Coroners are tempted to use it because of its definitive nature but this delays the identification of those whose bodies are intact. This approach forces families and friends to endure an unnecessarily long and painful wait over several days for definitive news. On top of this, human error can creep in, as in the case of the RAF Nimrod crash in Afghanistan in 2006, which killed fourteen military personnel. It was Britain's biggest single loss since the Falklands War. On April 29 2007 The Guardian reported: "Body parts of British soldiers who died on operations in Afghanistan have been mixed up and placed in the wrong coffins. The government has admitted that the remains of at least one serviceman, who died in Britain's worst military disaster in the war, ended up inside another victim's coffin."

The mistake occurred when someone on the identification team swabbed a finger with a wedding ring covered in someone else's blood. No one took a tissue sample. The parents were extremely gracious about the error: "We are both grateful that DNA identification was available and that we got some of our son back, but it must be done thoroughly."

The nightmare of mis-identification is one that plagues me to this day, so of course I understand Coroners' desires for accuracy but this worry has sometimes led to an over-reliance on scientific means of identification, the use of which (and the delays) sometimes fly in the face of common sense and compassion, in circumstances when people can be visually identified.

As Pam Dix wrote of her own experience: "Many [at Lockerbie] were identified by fingerprints and dental records even when they were fully recognisable, as in my brother's case, when he was travelling with his US Green card in his pocket (which has a full face photo, Social Security number and fingerprint on it). Seventeen people remained unidentified even though there were three intact male bodies and a set number of missing men. Six weeks after the crash the unidentified remains were cremated and buried. It would not have occurred to us then that this meant their identifications would never be possible. The loss is all the more acute for the lack of physical certainty, but in any case it takes years for the feeling that one day you might see him at the door, or in the street, to fade away."

On the other hand, one person remained unidentified after King's Cross fire of 1987 in which 31 people died but, in 2004, having been buried, his remains were exhumed and his identity restored to him through the use of DNA. DNA could perhaps help this person, speaking about the UTA 722 air crash that took place in Niger, 1989, when an international passenger flight operating from Brazzaville in the People's Republic of the Congo, via N'Djamena in Chad, to Charles de Gaulle Airport in Paris was brought down by a bomb detonated over the Sahara desert. All 156 passengers and 14 crew died: "My brother was never identified. Nor was it made clear that the body which might have been his was buried in Paris at the foot of the UTA Memorial, quite a big piece of ground. There was a small chance that he was not buried there, though his body was recovered. I think the odds were against that. I was offered a body as his in November 1989 and rejected it on the grounds that this suit shoe size was too small and the body was wearing heavy metal jewellery, such as I'd never see my brother wear."

Of course, DNA can now prevent terrible mistakes. As one woman, whose husband who died in a plane crash, wrote: "My husband was buried. A few months later, I was told that the parents of one of the British air hostesses had been given some of her jewellery that had been on the body, only it wasn't of their daughter; in other words they had buried the wrong body! I was asked if I wanted to take this further. I refused as I felt I did not want to go down a very painful route."

And in the other extreme, political pressure can lead to the rushing of identification. The Polish Air Force TU 154 crash in April 2010 in which 96 people died, including the President of Poland Lech Kaczyński, was not handled well. As one relative put it: "The fact that the investigation is being carried out by a foreign state has meant that mistakes have been made in identifications and exhumations have been necessary. I believe that there was political pressure to have identification completed as quickly as possible at the sacrifice of carrying out DNA in the majority of cases. This led to great distress and the need to exhume victims."

And sometimes DNA would have removed the chance for relatives to say goodbye: "If DNA testing had been available to identify the dead in 1987 it is likely that I would have been denied the chance to identify my brother myself, visually, which is what I did as he lay on a trolley in the corridor of a mortuary. I found that seeing him was psychologically extremely beneficial as it helped me to understand with certainty what had happened to him, and grasped that he was no longer there. It was also good to have a last moment to spend with him before he was buried ... It was important to me that I have been involved and alongside him as it were in the last part of my brother's journey even after he died. It felt like other people whom he didn't know were dealing with him and just processing him otherwise. What might have been helpful was a degree of preparation before I saw him. I felt terrified not knowing at all what kind of state he was going to be in."

Preparation for viewing is something I have always argued for. As another unprepared relative told Disaster Action: "The time lapse and damage, particularly to his face meant that his body was almost unrecognisable to me and seeing him in this state even for a few seconds has left a lasting and horrifying impression."

A parent speaking about the Manchester air disaster of 1985 told Disaster Action: "When I think of the difference the use of DNA would have made to families in the spate of disasters in the 1980s – they would have been a huge saving in unnecessary pain and suffering. We had to wait five days before our daughter was formally identified because they had to have a minimum number of criteria to agree before they would confirm the death... Because they refuse to release the names of victims until all had been identified (the result of bodies being identified with the wrong name), we had to wait an extra three days for the dentist to come back from holiday to confirm the dental records of another victim."

And there are always things that can catch you out. In relation to the London underground bombings of 2005: "For us, being asked for DNA samples by a police family liaison officer was an acknowledgement that our concerns about our son's involvement were real ones and being taken seriously. This is in marked contrast to the initial attitude of the Help Line and the three days we had to endure of remarks like "Oh he'll turn up," and questions like: "Does he often go off without telling you?"... Taking DNA samples was handled very sensitively. More problematic for me were other aspects of the identification process – for example, a family dentist was contacted without consulting us and this was very upsetting for staff there who had known my son since he was four years old but had not realised his involvement in 7/7 at that stage."

During a DVI operation, information has to be carefully controlled. I heard of many cases where families found out intimate details about their loved ones from the media. Even worse are other kinds of leaks, such as occurred after the Polish Air Force Flight TU154: "Recently pictures of bodies from the crash site had been leaked on the Internet. The photos were taken by someone officially at the site and cover bodies at the site, bodies in coffins before they were sealed and bodies at the morgue. These pictures identified the persons photographed. Such things should never have been allowed to occur. Aside from naming individuals we have experienced their voices being played at press conferences. In our case there seems to be little understanding as to the trauma events such as this cause ... I feel sometimes that no public disclosures should be made at all until the investigation is closed and permission from affected families has been obtained."

As Eyre and Dix write: "The impact of the often impersonal and invasive process that leads to an identification can be profound and long-lasting on those left behind." If there was one thing I'd learned from looking at the work and experiences of Disaster Action, it was that DVI required one to never forget that you were doing this for the victims' families – and keeping their best interests at heart meant that one always had to remain flexible.

TWELVE

WHEN SUICIDE IS MURDER

9.30pm, Saturday 6th November 2004. I was standing beside another railway line. At my feet, lit by arc lights, was the intact body of a nine-year-old girl and, nearby the body of the man responsible for her death. Everything else, the huge crash site, the flashing red and blue lights of more than twenty emergency vehicles, the shouts of rescue workers, all had faded into the background. Eventually, I realised someone was calling my name.

"Dick? Dick, we have to move her. We have to, for dignity's sake."

* * *

An off-duty police officer, Police Constable Mark Brazier spotted the silver Mazda stopped between the barriers on the level crossing that served a narrow lane that linked the village of Ufton Nervet to the Bath Road (the A4), seven miles west of Reading in Berkshire, at about 6.10pm.

Automatic half-barrier level crossings (AHB) are a common sight on the UK's smaller country roads, where the rail line-speed is less than 100mph, places where there's never any traffic congestion. The idea of the AHB is that while they close the road to approaching traffic, they also allow any vehicle still crossing when the barriers come down to escape. Unfortunately, this doesn't prevent road users in a hurry from zigzagging through the crossing when the barriers are down. The automatic half-barrier equipment at Ufton Nervet, between Theale and Aldermaston rail stations was in good condition and properly maintained on the evening of November 6 2004.

Inside the silver Mazda was 48-year-old chef Bryan Drysdale, who worked at the nearby luxury Wokefield Park Hotel. Drysdale had left early, claiming he was feeling ill.

PC Brazier watched as Drysdale manoeuvred his car until he was positioned with the vehicle side-on to the rails. Brazier flashed his lights and beeped his horn but got no response from Drysdale. Brazier then leapt of his car to shout at Drysdale to move the car – just as the crossing alarm sounded and the gates started to come down. Brazier tried to use the emergency phone at the crossing's side to warn controllers to halt the train. He expected it to work like emergency phones on motorways which automatically connected callers to a control room. Railway phones did not, however, and, as it was dark, and probably because of the extreme stress, he couldn't see the instructions.

Stanley Martin, 54, the driver of the InterCity 125 First Great Western service from London Paddington to Plymouth, with 281 people on board, was already too close. On a downward curve, he shut off power and coasted for around four seconds, normal for this point in the journey. After turning the corner that brought him in sight of the Ufton Nervet crossing at nearly 100mph, Martin, a driver with thirty years' experience, was only able to apply the brakes three seconds before impact.

Brazier turned his back as the train struck the car. He was showered with broken glass.

As it was, the train only clipped the car, as it was mainly on the London-bound side of the track but the impact was enough to derail the forward wagon, so that it travelled at about 25° to the rails, until reaching the points at the start of a loop, ninety metres beyond the crossing. At this point the forward power car derailed completely and jammed, stopping almost dead, and with the train's rear power car still at near full speed the train jack-knifed at its middle, destroying the silver Mazda as the 411-tonne, 200-metre long set of eight carriages folded, twisted, flipped and rolled.

One carriage was turned 360° while the family coach – where most passengers were sitting – slid along on its side. Passengers were tumbled over and onto one another as they were thrown down towards the smashed windows of this coach, one passenger felt his arm and then head go through the window but managed to pull his head back in, an action that saved his life.

When the post-crash silence filled the air, people got up, starting to look for a way out. But the lights had failed in some coaches and it was pitch black. People used mobile phones to try and light their way, seeing faces covered in blood looking back at hem, others unable to walk, crying for help, someone shouting about a broken arm, everything covered in broken glass.

In one carriage the train manager had been checking tickets; he shouted for people to hold still, in case movement caused the carriage to roll any further. He then switched on emergency lighting and made sure the carriage was stable before leading people to the doors.

Other passengers trapped in carriages needed to break windows to escape, but some of the safety hammers had been broken or lost in the crash, and then they faced the difficulty of getting to windows that were now – because the carriage was lying on its side – above their head.

Passengers helped one another to safety but had to leave those who were too badly injured to be moved, although some stayed – a son with his elderly mother and a father cradling his daughter, who had died.

The air was thick with diesel fumes. Someone, suffering shock, tried to light a cigarette and was quickly shouted down.

Injured passengers were first helped at the Winning Hand pub, right by the level crossing – and this is where the first paramedics arrived, fifteen minutes after the crash. The one lady who happened to be working there at the time fetched coffee, tea and water for the walking wounded, and a local man arrived to help and later arranged transport for people to get home.

Two men found the girl, thrown clear of the wreckage. She was nine years old. She had a head wound and was bleeding. They felt a weak pulse and did what they could to keep her alive.

* * *

I was at home in Rotherham when I received the call just before 6.30pm. Minutes later I was in my car, punching in the sat-nav coordinates for Ufton Nervet. Three hours. I was grateful for the time to think. To try and help me – and others- cope with the heat of those first moments, the on-scene arrival, I'd devised a forty-point checklist that fitted on two pages of A4 to make sure nothing was forgotten, and I talked myself through them as I drove.

I'd always admired the pathologists who worked at disaster scenes; they were disturbed by the carnage like anyone else but, used to fragmentation and the sight of internal organs, they were able to maintain an "at-ease" state of professionalism, so I tried to model my behaviour on the best of them. The absolute key to working successfully on disaster sites is trust and teamwork but I also had to accept that some people would not be able to remain professional at all times – emotions would sometimes take over; it's what makes us human.

I met Steve Gregory at the scene. Steve was an inspector with the Met and was my colleague in Disaster Management at Centrex. Steve provided training in mass fatality management, particularly with regard to initial scene attendance as well as command and control. He also had experience in victim recovery and between us we would be able to provide a good level of advice to the investigating force. Steve had arrived first and he briefed me as we walked.

"There are 120 injured, 61 of whom were badly hurt enough to require hospital treatment, they've been taken to the Royal Berkshire Hospital in Reading and the North Hampshire Hospital in Basingstoke. Twelve are serious."

"And the deceased?"

"Fire Brigade has suggested there might be six or seven, so far. They've cut eleven survivors from the wreckage and need to free some of the deceased too, once the DVI teams arrive."

More than twenty ambulances from five counties as well as fourteen fire engines were at the crash site. It looked like chaos but all the cordons were in place and I could tell everything had been handled well. Although this was under the jurisdiction of the British Transport Police who were yet to be trained in DVI, they were more than happy to have Steve and myself advise. I'd provided lots of DVI training to the provincial force, which was Thames Valley, thanks to their coordinator, Sergeant Gill Williams who specialised in underwater searches, and who became a good friend of mine.

And then I saw the wreckage. The scale took my breath away. You forget just how big those carriages are. To see them out of their usual context, strewn like children's toys across fields and tracks was a real shock.

"Unbelievable to think anyone could have survived, let alone walked away," I said. "Do we know the cause?"

"Car was on the level crossing when the barriers were down. Could be a suicide. Train jack-knifed in the middle; the middle carriage is where most injuries and fatalities are. People were thrown out of the windows; could be more under the train."

An utterly senseless act, I thought. No one here should have died today.

"Train driver alive?"

Steve shook his head. "Fire brigade's ready to free him now. I'll show you the scene."

We passed the silver Mazda on the way, or what was left of it. Just the chassis and framework.

Every mass fatality is treated as a homicide until proven otherwise but this one really looked as though it was a crime. If he had survived, the driver of the car would have certainly been prosecuted for manslaughter, probably murder.

My adrenaline levels soared as Steve took me through the scene and I breathed in the familiar smell of diesel. Well, I thought, my nerves have certainly kicked in; I wonder when my professionalism will follow?

And then we found ourselves in front of the dead girl.

"And we think that's the driver of the car."

He was lying nearby. Their bodies were mainly intact. As always, it's the intact bodies that are harder to deal with. I knew then that I was never going to get used to this job, to seeing the dead and that anyone in this line of work would always be out-side of their comfort zone.

Steve wanted the girl moved, for dignity's sake. We couldn't leave her lying there all night, he argued. It was against my DVI procedures but I agreed in this case that for her family's sake and for the sake of the people working here, it was best to move her as soon as possible, before the DVI team briefing. Steve and I decided to handle the recovery, after clearing it with the SIM from the British Transport Police. This was the first time we used the new ACPO victim label. We tied the scene label to a fence near to where the girl had died, and recovered her using a waiting ambulance.

This time we had a trained team and it was during the briefing that my professional-self awoke.

"No sirs or titles in DVI," I told them, "We'll use first names. And although I'm the go-to guy for advice, I'm just as fallible as anyone else. If you don't feel something is right. If you think I've missed something, then tell me."

This, I felt, had the beneficial effect of empowering people to question what was happening, which in turn would help me be a better adviser in the future. Nevertheless, I could see plenty of nervous people in front of me and I could feel the apprehension. This was the ultimate de-selection course. You only know – truly know – when you're deployed.

I would go on to train 4,000 people in DVI. Less than five per cent of them will ever use their training in a real life scenario but everyone has to be as prepared as they can be. I warn my trainees that despite the odds being against them ever having to use the skills I'd taught them, they should never forget what they'd learned, and should regularly go over the literature, re-read their notes because: "If a disaster does take place on your patch, when the Assistant Chief Constable is looking at list of the people he/she needs to call, he/she will see an asterisk next to your name and that means you will be expected to perform to the standards that have been set, no excuses. Don't have nightmares about this, just re-read the literature and take my phone number, along with all the other MDAT phone numbers because, if you do get the call then you will want to call someone for advice and support."

We spent most of the night at the scene, recovering the victims and body parts, waiting for some hours while the fire brigade worked on the delicate job of freeing the dead. The driver's cab had completely filled with ballast and earth that had poured through broken windows as the engine-car had ploughed into the ground. Firemen worked with cranes to lift an entire carriage so that we could reach a victim who had been half-thrown out of a window before the carriage had rolled on top of them. After that, each carriage was lifted in turn, to make sure we hadn't missed anything. The crash, investigation and repairs would block the line – the main railway route between London and the West Country – for almost ten days, until the morning of November 16.

All of the deceased were taken to the Royal Berkshire hospital. As was usual, I would always lead the process for the first victim, to remind people of their training, talking my way through everything I was doing. By the time that was done any of my team would be ready to leap into the saddle for the next victim, having recalled their training and found their confidence now that the first had been processed. It's not rocket science, it's procedure and once they've seen one and done one, I should no longer be needed. This was what the training was all about.

We examined the girls, aged nine and fourteen, first. A full autopsy was at this time routine, even when it clearly wasn't necessary. I debated the issue with the Coroner, arguing the case that such procedures were unnecessary and invasive, a secondary assault and he agreed, instructing the pathologist to only conduct an external examination on the two girls and the three other passengers. The drivers of the train and the car would have full autopsies and toxicology tests to make sure there were no other factors that contributed to the accident.

Although this was a benchmark case (this was the first time it was decided not to perform a full autopsy after an accident/ sudden death to determine cause), the Coroner always has the final say. In terms of DVI an invasive autopsy is only helpful when we needed help with identification in cases where things like prosthetics, pacemakers, unique medical conditions etc., would be helpful. To get to the bottom of the cause of a crash like this, it is necessary to perform autopsies on the bodies of those who were in control of the crash vehicles. The decision made here was replicated in the wake of 7/7 where clearly blast injuries were the cause of death. There is a fine line though. The Coroner who examined the charred bodies of the people who died in the Manchester jumbo jet fire found they died from asphyxiation because they couldn't get out quickly enough. This led to compulsory low-level lighting on all airplane floors so people can find their way out. If the autopsy hadn't been invasive we would not have known.

There is a possibility that while families will appreciate the sensitivity of not conducting a full autopsy, such a decision may, in some cases, lead to families asking questions that could only be answered by a post mortem. In other words, there are many ways one can die from "blast injuries" and some relatives might want to know the details of how their loved one died. It may be that some people would feel that shortcuts were being taken or that not everything was done that should have been done in the name of thoroughness, or perhaps feel that information was being deliberately withheld.

I tend to come down on the side of a full autopsy in most cases as we stand to learn more that way. It's about making things better for the living (autopsies can even reveal genetic conditions that the family may not have known about) – but there are definitely times when it's not necessary.

As we searched and undressed the two girls, the atmosphere grew tense. Everyone was maintaining a professional exterior but I could feel the human, emotional side that everyone was struggling to contain. I knew only too well how hard it was to maintain this balance. I myself often felt like the proverbial swan; in control on the surface while my legs were paddling like fury underneath. We can tell ourselves to leave our emotions outside the mortuary door but it's so hard when you start to find out about that person's life, you pull out a library card from someone's pocket and suddenly you have a name. The secret to dealing with this is to be aware of the humanity of the person but to hold yourself distant while you're processing their body. After the incident, it's almost inevitable that DVI officers will come across articles and news clips that feature the accident and the people involved, or interviews with the families of the deceased, and it helps to be ready for this. Part of being ready is feeling positive about what you've done to help the families. Some find it hard to understand that DVI is, despite its sad and gruesome nature, "rewarding" work. You're there to help the families. Of course, it's not easy, and you won't receive thanks (at least not specific thanks – families often thank the rescue services in statements released to the press), as you're doing something that's simply expected to be done, and rightly so. Plus it's very much an unknown side of police work. But it's not about the thanks. It's understandable that when people have lost someone they love, they just want them back and they want closure. They are so deep in grief that they don't need to acknowledge how that happens.

When I see people being drawn into the emotional side of their work in the mortuary, I try to refocus them, to take them away from those human aspects of the person we're working with, to focus on the job. And in this case, once we had dealt with the children, I suggested we downed tools and talk. Being a cop I'm able to penetrate other cops' defence systems.

In this case however, with the body of the suicide victim on the next table someone said: "He might have taken his own life but he murdered six innocent people." There was definitely a feeling that he didn't deserve any dignity. I could even feel my own judgement coming into play but I knew that this was base emotion. I decided to stop proceedings once more. "Remember why we're here and what we're doing. We're not working for him," I said, pointing at the suicide victim, "We're working for his family. They are innocent and they deserve our full professional attention."

I was exhausted by the time we'd finished. I'd stayed all night at the scene while the bodies were recovered and then worked all day in the mortuary with the identification teams. I'd worked too long and this was a reminder for me to take breaks every now and again. It doesn't help to have an exhausted member of staff. The reason I drove myself so hard was because I know that while families appreciate how hard our job sometimes is, and that we are constrained by time-consuming procedures, as time goes by this understanding can turn into resentment, especially if they have to wait for their loved one to be officially identified and therefore to see and be with them. Apart from the loss of trust and cooperation and bad publicity (pressure from the media), it is vitally important psychologically for the families to know that their loved one has been identified and is a step closer to being returned to them. Excuses about logistics will not suffice. As I shall explain in the next chapter, viewing at a funeral director's after the release of the body some days is not the same as viewing the body as soon as possible after identification.

All of the six victims were successfully ID'd – the seventh died in hospital the following day but still went through the DVI process – and I was impressed by the DVI team's awareness of procedures as well as their handling of the new Victim Identification Forms.

Anyone who's ever worked with me on DVI will know of my dislike for the unnecessarily complex Interpol forms, which are essentially a set of documents used to record the results of the various stages of examination. As an Interpol member country, we were signed up to the Interpol Standing Committees DVI resolution to use this form in the case of a mass fatality when it was suspected that foreign nationals were involved. This meant that ante- and post-mortem data could cross international boundaries and all nations would share a common understanding of the manner in which the data was presented.

While I accept the use of these forms when foreign nationals are involved in a disaster, I learned, after Dunkeswick and Selby (which only involved UK citizens) that these forms could be improved upon for UK use. In other words we could spend much less time on bureaucracy and more on actual identification work.

In 2002, I came up with the idea for an alternative set of mortuary forms to be used after a 'domestic' mass fatality incident. Over the next two years, burning much midnight oil, and with the help of Karon whose technical know-how saved me from the hell of computer-aided design, the ACPO Victim Profile Forms were introduced in July 2004. They were a set of colour-coded forms, with each colour relating to a separate part of the mortuary examination. More user-friendly and efficient, the information could, where necessary, be transferred to an Interpol form, should one of the victims turn out to be a foreign national. The Ufton Nervet rail crash was our first chance to put them into practice, and after plenty of positive feedback, they were instated as an alternative option for the SIM.

The post-mortem revealed that the train driver had died of asphyxiation from the earth that had filled his cab after the windows had broken. And of course, it was impossible to avoid the ensuing news reports and the subsequent inquest that filled in the details of my own experience that November night.

Although the high structural integrity of the Mark 3 train coaches prevented a much higher death toll plus the fact that the sparsely filled first-class coaches were at the leading end of the train, most of the dead suffered severe head injuries after being thrown from the train through broken windows. This knowledge assisted the families in their call for improved safety at the inquest, for trains to be fitted with laminated glass, which is more resistant in crash situations. The laminated glass windscreen of the front power car remained unbroken, for example, but the weaker side window of the cab, made from toughened glass, shattered like many of the carriage windows, and the cab filled with ballast and earth. The surviving parents of the deceased children believed that had laminated glass been fitted, their children would have survived. This change was by then already being made by the rail company.

Drysdale's car was uninsured and unreliable but Forensic Accident Investigator David Price reported that the car's engine had been switched off, that the handbrake was fully applied, that the vehicle's lights were switched off, that the steering was on a partial left hand lock and that the fuel tank contained eight litres – about two gallons- of petrol.

Dr. Philip Joseph, a consultant forensic psychiatrist who examined Drysdale's mental, medical and personal history, reported that the chef was "tormented by his homosexuality," something he'd concealed from friends and some of his family. Just days earlier, Drysdale had phoned NHS Direct, saying he thought he might have HIV after a one-night stand with a man five years before. He also said that he had suicidal thoughts and described feeling "his head cracking," before adding: "I think I'm having a bit of a nervous breakdown to be honest." He called the hospital where he'd been tested for HIV on November 6.

We didn't know this during the mortuary process. Obviously there had been major risk to mortuary and DVI staff but this lack of knowledge was the norm in disaster response. We have no idea about the medical history of the people in our body bags and although we try to measure the levels of risk and necessary caution against the speed with which we need to work, we can never really know what we might be dealing with in terms of communicable diseases.

The clinic was closed Saturdays, so Drysdale couldn't get through. The test would come back negative. Dr. Joseph said Drysdale may have believed he was dying of AIDS and was, by parking on the level crossing, merely accelerating the process. As to whether he planned to take others with him, that seemed unlikely but clearly he was not in a fit mental state to consider the harm his actions would cause to others.

Then came the families. David Main lost his partner and his daughter in the accident and talked about the pain and loss he'd experienced from the moment he realised they were dead. They had meant to take an earlier train but instead ended up on the 5.35pm service from Paddington. David had been waiting to meet them at Newbury station.

Passenger Brian Kemsley described how he found them, mother Anjanette Rossi and daughter Louella, lying beside the wreckage. Louella died as he tried to save her. A vicar who'd also been travelling on the train said a prayer with Brian over her body.

Peter Webster was sitting opposite his 14-year-old-daughter Emily and her friend Christine when the crash happened. Emily died, Peter held her in his arms for some time, amidst the wreckage. Christine was left trapped but survived.

On-board data recording equipment made it clear Stanley Martin had done everything possible to avert the accident and, on what would have been his 55th birthday, First Great Western named power car 43139 after him. Today there is a small "Area of Reflection" close to the crossing, with two wooden benches facing an engraved steel memorial plaque remembering all the people affected by the collision.

The deceased were: Passengers Barry Strevens, 55, from Wells, Somerset; Emily Webster, 14, from Moretonhampstead, Devon; Anjanette Rossi, 38, from Speen, Berkshire, and her daughter, Louella Main, nine. Brian Drysdale, 48, of Reading, Berkshire (the car driver) Stanley Martin, 54, from Torquay. Leslie Matthews, 72, from Warminster, Wiltshire, died in hospital the following day.

A support network, the Ufton Nervet Train Crash Network was set up for survivors and relatives of the victims and in November 2014, candles were lit and a minute's silence was held at the Area of Reflection next to the site at the exact time of the crash to mark the tenth anniversary of the tragedy. The Ufton Nervet rail crossing remains in place despite a further four deaths since the rail crash – the most recent taking place in October 2014 when Gary Provins, 60, from Calcot, was struck by a train- but Network Rail has said that work was about to start on building a bridge over the line.

***

The year 2004 had been a groundbreaking year for DVI. I had trained hundreds – soon to be thousands – of officers in DVI and disasters were being better handled as a result. Coroners had stopped ordering autopsies for every incident, using sound judgement based on advice from experts at the scene. Setting the scientific parameters of what exactly constituted human remains had, along with training, helped speed up identification and res-titution, and at the same time the families would always be kept fully updated about what we were doing. There was one issue where there seemed to be no recognised protocol, however, and that was the viewing of the deceased.

THIRTEEN

VIEWING THE DECEASED

In terms of identification, facial recognition by relatives can be problematic for DVI work. The face or/and body of a dead body does not necessarily look as the person was in life. Even small post-mortem changes, such as hair, expression or skin colour, can cause someone to doubt whom they're seeing. Also, viewing a deceased relative comes with a host of psychological issues; the viewer does not necessarily want to believe what they're being shown, for example, or in the opposite case, they are 'hopeful' that their loved one's body has been found and want to have the closure they've been aching for. Many mis-identifications can be made under these circumstances.

Although I'm in favour of showing relatives the body of their loved one whenever possible, and we should never deny a viewing if requested – after having talked them through the process and preparing them with a gently delivered verbal description or maybe even a photograph of what they're about to see – there are times (in cases of extreme fragmentation or decomposition, for example) when it is simply not appropriate. Viewing trauma and decomposition of a human body is distressing enough for experienced professionals, let alone for a relative who might not have ever seen a dead body before.

To that end, recent scientific developments have allowed forensic artists, either through sketching, or the use of computer software such as Adobe Photoshop, using anatomical knowledge and an understanding of the effects of decomposition, to eliminate a great deal of the trauma, discolouration and decomposition and recreate the victim's face as it was in life. In cases where we just have a skull then something called facial approximation can be used to recreate the face by relating the skeletal structure to the overlying soft tissue. It's an amazing technique that has been successfully used in forensic identifications across the globe. Another method available to the identification team is cranio-facial superimposition, which is the comparison of the skull with ante-mortem photographs. The image of the skull and the image of the person are superimposed – scaling is achieved by using teeth or external objects in the image of the suspect such as jewellery or furniture- and, with careful measurement and comparison, this can be reliable tool for identification teams. Cranio-facial superimposition was used to help identify victims of Fred and Rosemary West, the serial killers who murdered at least eleven girls in Gloucester between 1967 and 1987.

One side effect of the increasing use of scientific methods of identification is that relatives now have little, if any, involvement in the processing of the deceased after a disaster. It's quite rare that relatives are needed to identify the deceased because we now have reliable well-established scientific methods that we can rely upon. Often the body is released to the family, after lengthy delays, from the custody of the Coroner, simply ready for burial or cremation. Psychologically, this is too late for many relatives to spend time with the deceased, to be a part of their final journey. Also, I had noticed that there was little evidence to guide professionals working with bereaved relatives after a sudden traumatic death and, as I had seen, approaches by the police to bereaved families varied wildly from the over-protective to almost indifferent.

In the UK, where closed-casket burials have been the norm since the middle of the 20th Century, we've become used to not seeing dead bodies. We tend to fear corpses, especially because we're taught that a dead body is dangerous; it leaks fluids that contain bacteria and, possibly, contagious diseases. This fear is amplified in the case of traumatic death, where disfigurement – often extreme – has taken place. Professionals will argue against families and friends seeing people in such states, believing that this will lead to unpleasant memories and nightmares. And, although there are no rules about who can touch a dead body, Coroners will withhold the body from family and friends if a criminal offence is suspected, so that no evidence is lost. On occasion, in my opinion, some Coroners have gone to far. After the Lockerbie bombing, the procurator fiscal (who acts as Coroner in Scotland) did not allow bereaved relatives access to the bodies until they had been identified using dental records and fingerprints. Funeral directors were then instructed that it would be better for the relatives if they did not see the bodies. Pam Dix had been told that her brother was intact and fully recognisable. She asked to see his body at the crematorium but was told this was against regulations and "medically inadvisable." Pam was left distraught and bitter about her treatment.

Obviously, a sudden loss is extremely hard to come to terms with. It has been argued that confronting the unshakeable reality of a dead body helps makes a sudden loss real and makes it possible for the survivor to sever bonds with the deceased person so they can eventually move on. Other researchers argue that these bonds do not have to be severed and in fact viewing the body helps maintain the bond they had in life, which is helpful when going through the lengthy logistical process of losing a loved one.

When researchers interviewed bereaved relatives after the 1987 Zeebrugge ferry disaster, in which 193 people died, between three and twelve months after the tragedy, they found that people who had viewed the bodies of their deceased relatives felt worse in terms distress and anxiety than those who had not. They repeated the study two years later and found that the viewers' distress and anxiety about the incident had decreased to levels below those who did not view. They also found that there was no significant distress/anxiety difference between those people who had viewed more disrupted bodies and those whose who had viewed bodies in a 'normal' state.

Ultimately, we do not know and should not judge what people want or need when their loved ones have died as a result of a disaster. Nor will they until 'it happens' and each person will react differently. Where people still believe that the police will require them to identify the body, they need to be told that this is simply not the case. Many people want to see the body of their loved one, and the reasons are surprisingly varied.

When I first met with Disaster Action I became especially interested in viewing, as there was no research into the viewing of the deceased by the relatives for identification and psychological purposes. But in April 2010, a paper published in the British Medical Journal (*Viewing the body after bereavement due to a traumatic death: qualitative study in the UK*, Alison Chapple and Sue Ziebland) reported on the cases of eighty people who had suffered a sudden bereavement, a suicide or other traumatic death. It confirmed my own thoughts and provided statements from people who had been through the process, and I quote from these statements here.

As to people's motivations for viewing the body of their loved one; first and foremost, as far as I am concerned, it is to make sure that there hasn't been a mistake.

Rachel's son, Dave, was killed by a bomb in Iraq. In this case the Coroner asked if Rachel could assist in identifying her son's body. Rachel agreed because she wanted to be certain it was indeed him. When she arrived at the mortuary, before the viewing she asked a technician if she would recognise her son. "No, I don't think you will," was the reply. "He doesn't look like he does on that passport." Rachel said this was a bit of a shock, and I would agree this is not the best way to receive that information. It needs to be volunteered from the Coroner, and the condition explained.

When Rachel was asked if she'd done the right thing by going in to see Dave she replied: "Most definitely, yes, yes, I had to make sure that that was my son, because you know, they might have made a mistake."

Mothers and fathers are obviously used to caring for their children and of course these feelings do not stop at the moment a parent learns that their child is dead they do not refer to them as 'a body', for example. There is a need to care. People often say that they need to see their loved one as soon as possible to make sure they are "alright." Unfortunately, some families have to wait because of the need to collect forensic evidence before the post-mortem examination. A police officer or the Coroner's officer will frequently insist on observing the viewing, for continuity (forensic) reasons. Having to wait to see a deceased loved one is impossibly distressing. Doubts as to whether it was their child combined with the need to care for them if it is – and then being watched when one is finally allowed to see them, at what should be a time of intimacy; all this can only compound the distress. There is an unshakeable need for people to comfort their loved ones after they've died. For example, Jayne's husband was murdered by a schizophrenic.

"And when they took me into Jon, where Jon was laid out, you know, he was in a room on his own and I think my, my over-riding feeling was that I didn't want Jon to be frightened (...). I know it's going to sound a bit silly, but I think the over-riding feeling was that I wanted to share, I can't say share what he was experiencing but be there with him so that he wasn't on his own.

So I talked to him a lot, and I reassured him that he wasn't on his own, and sang to him."

Elizabeth's daughter was killed in a car accident: "I just wanted to get to her straightaway because I felt that there was something I could do. That's what every mother feels, isn't it, you can always do something to make it better."

Pat had to wait for eight hours before she could see her son: "I wished that it had been a shorter period of time. I think, as his mother, I wanted to be with him, and of course we want to be with our, our children through their important experiences. (...) But of course the Coroner's officer, and I guess it's a rule of some sort, but she came into the place with me and was standing on the other side of a glass, a small glass screen where she could see me the whole time. So I wasn't allowed to be with Matthew, with my son on my own. And I am sorry about that and I don't understand why it is that a mother cannot be with her child on her own if that's what she wishes. I don't understand why I could not have washed him, I could not have dressed him, I could not have looked after him (...) it feels like the organisation, the state, whatever it is, the police authorities, had taken my son and were doing with him what they felt best to do. And I was suddenly an outsider and not able to do things for my son (...) It felt as if he was somebody else's property and I had to ask permission to go and see him. And I had to be observed whilst I did."

Margaret's daughter hanged herself: "The Coroner's officer said, "We can't stop you, we can't prevent you because that's your right. But we would strongly advise that you wait until the funeral director has seen to your daughter before you see her." And I can remember saying, "Well she's my daughter, she doesn't need to look pretty, I need to hold her." ... I was terrified that she might still be lingering around her body in a confused state because of the suddenness of the death."

Helen who lost her daughter Charlotte: "I felt at the time, and I still feel, that it was the most important thing that I needed to do... I would've regretted for the rest of my life if I hadn't have done that. ... I sat next to Charlotte for, I don't remember, maybe fifteen minutes, and I spoke to her. I think it, it was more important than at the funeral, saying goodbye actually, because she, I could see her."

Clearly, it's important to us all to be as close to our loved ones' bodies as soon as possible after they have died. This is much harder after a major disaster when scenes need to be cleared and forensic evidence collected. Families are always sympathetic with regards to our job, but this sympathy understandably starts to quickly fade once 24hours have passed.

People have also said they wanted to see the body so that they could put their imaginations to rest, i.e., reality is not as bad as one's imagination. Marion's husband committed suicide in 1996. He had done this through carbon monoxide poisoning and when Marion saw his body she didn't recognise him. Despite this, she went back to see his body again with her four children who were aged ten to 22. She strongly believed this was the right decision.

"I don't remember asking them if they wanted to see the body. I remember them telling me they wanted to. I don't know whether I'd have had the courage to ask them to be honest, but they both said, "Where is he? What's happening to him and what does he look like?" And then the older, the middle one saying, "Well I want to see him." And then the other one of course said, "Well I do as well." Not to be left out. I know my, my parents particularly were absolutely horrified that I'd allowed them to do that. With the benefit of hindsight I would do it again. It would never occur to me now not to. Afterwards I thought, "Oh I shouldn't have done that. The trauma of them seeing him like that," but maybe the trauma of what they would have imagined would have been worse."

Others want to be with their loved one's body out of a sense of duty. Some religions (Hinduism, for example) require relatives to wash the body of the deceased, while others require an open coffin.

Even when there's disruption or decomposition, people still want to see the body of their loved one and believe that it was the right thing to do. Rachel saw her son's body after it came back from Iraq: "... even though he had lots of injuries and, you know, he had a massive like head injury and had snapped his leg, and all down his left side was completely injured, sort of squashed was a better word for it, but it was still him."

And then there is that need to have the reality brought home, spending time with the body can help stop part of the disbelief. Sarah's husband, Russell, was injured in a car crash and died in the operating theatre. "The fact that having actually seen him dead is the reality-check that makes you realise, "No this is the real world, he has gone." ... It's part of being able to believe that he is dead because if I hadn't seen him I think the being able to believe he is dead would have been much harder."

Although this reality-check can help, it is always important for those who are experienced in viewing the dead to brief the family and friends of the deceased as to the state of the body, so that they can prepare themselves, so that there is less of a shock at the moment of viewing.

Marcus identified his fiancée after she had been stabbed to death. He asked to see her again, before she was cremated, so he could say goodbye: "Louise's face was very badly bruised, and it was so many different colours. And her hair was sort of matted. They tried their best to make her look like we remembered her. But it didn't... it wasn't her.... If you can imagine this is after a number of weeks, almost months, she was a lot of different colours. She was black, green, brown, purple. And I kissed her on the forehead, and, and said goodbye that way. So for me it was...

"What would you've liked the funeral director to have said?"

"I guess in a way it would've been good if he'd said, "She's not going to look how you remember so please take that into consideration," rather than just let me in. I suppose in looking back I might've known what she was going to look like. I'm not, I'm not silly or stupid. But I thought she might look a bit more, I don't know, like how she used to look asleep. But she didn't."

"Are you glad you saw her?"

"I wouldn't change that for the world. I'm pleased I saw her. And I'm pleased in a way I could only see her face and not all the brutality that had happened to her."

People who regret seeing their loved ones seem to be in the minority (about one per cent). Sally was asked by police to identify her mother who had died in a fire after her brother failed to recognise her. Sally didn't want to do this but felt obliged: "So, yes, so I had to, I saw her and I knew it was her and I just literally, one second and then, because I just thought I can't have that look, that thought, in my head all the time of her. And I think that was probably the worst part, I think of the whole scenario actually, was actually seeing her. I wish I hadn't done that. That was the worst experience actually, and personally I'd never do that, again. I'd avoid seeing any dead body because I think that was awful."

As well as the type of death, the opinions of others (friends, family, professionals) were a major influence about whether to view a body. In the study, eight people had decided not to view the body of their dead friend or relative. Rosemary was asked by a Family Liaison Officer if she wanted to identify her son's body after he was killed in the London bombing of 2005. She opted for DNA, but wondered afterwards if she had made the right decision.

"My sister-in-law, who has been involved in this kind of area, said, "Don't, definitely don't [identify the body] because you don't need to do that, and in the circumstances it will be an appallingly difficult thing for you to do." ... But I still wonder, if I'm really honest, whether I should have done [identified the body] but I'm not sure ... I'm ambivalent about it because part of me feels that it's not closure, because it's not about that where I'm concerned, it's about understanding the reality of what happened and I'm not sure that if you don't do that [identify the body] whether you really do. ... My feeling still is that we made the right decision because that isn't the right way to remember somebody, I don't think, it really isn't."

Writing in the British Medical Journal, Sheila Awoonor-Renner[5] described how her 17-year-old son died in an accident and emergency department. She believes that – as far as hospital emergency room deaths go – that parents should immediately be given a choice over what to do next, to be involved. This reinforces the parent/child bond, that the parent 'owns' the child (as opposed to the Coroner) and has the right to care for them.

I agree with this and, based on the other research summarised above, it's extremely important for us to provide a place where families can see and be with their loved one's body after death as soon as they have been identified. This should be done in such a way – handled by FLOs with someone from the mortuary-so that DVI-related work can continue on other bodies, and work on identifying other bodies isn't delayed or interfered with. It's always possible that some families will visit the emergency mortuary whether viewing facilities are available or not ; although viewing facilities are always supposed to be available, there may be occasions when there hasn't been enough time to set them up, or the nature of the disaster makes their use inadvisable. It has happened. If this is the case, then they should not be made to feel

---

5 Awoonor-Renner S. Managing sudden bereavement, BMJ 1992; 304:1566

like unwelcome visitors, as has also happened, as this will only add to their distress.

It's clear from the above that families will want to see the body of their loved one, whatever state it might be in before it is returned to them 'officially', perhaps via a funeral director, by which time it will be ready for burial or cremation. Every effort should be made to help the families exercise this right as clearly, it's important for their future psychological well-being.

Back in November 2004, after successfully dealing with three incidents and their aftermath in ten months, I really felt as though I was starting to make a difference. I then made the mistake of thinking I was ready for anything.

FOURTEEN

THE WAVE

I was really looking forward to Christmas. I was happily settled with Karon, had a fantastically interesting and satisfying job, training people in DVI, based out of the National Centre of Police Excellence (NCPE) and, for the first time in years, I wasn't going to be working. The NCPE allowed Christmas and Boxing Day off, although you were always on call for any advisory role. As I had had such a busy year in terms of DVI with three incidents in ten months and an ever-increasing training programme, I felt that it wouldn't be too much to trust fate with my two-day break.

So, apart from a family Christmas Day set in my sights, I was eagerly anticipating the traditional Boxing Day ritual for most blokes – watching a good footy match and that year, my club Rotherham, aka the Millers were away to Leicester. My passion for the Millers knows no bounds. As a constable I'd always volunteered to work overtime patrolling the footy when the Millers were at home and in 1978 they drew Arsenal in the Cup. I ended up policing the Arsenal end and, unfortunately, abandoned all professionalism when Rotherham's third goal went in. Jubilant to the point of euphoria, I threw my helmet into the air, just about causing a riot.

Christmas Day was as it is for any other family but I was soaking up the fact that I was home for once and able to enjoy it. And then, on Boxing Day, after delighting in the rare luxury of a lie in, we got ready for the match.

In 2004, Rotherham were again flying high – for them – and enjoying life in the Championship. I was full of high hopes when we set off for the Walker Stadium with Karon and my son Matt – and as Karon was driving – I was looking forward to having a few beers to add to the festive sociability. As expected, the atmosphere was extremely festive, with both sides brimming with optimism for their team. At 2.50pm I was in the public bar, having just bought a pre-match beer in preparation for the 3pm kick-off. I raised the drink to my lips.

And then my phone rang.

I couldn't hear whatever it was the other person was trying to tell me. The teams had emerged and the crowds were trying to outdo each other's chants. After a few seconds I realised that the man on the other end was Dick Woodman, a Detective Superintendent from the Met who had been on my most recent SIM course, which had taken place earlier in December.

"Dick, I've been appointed SIM for an incident that's taken place outside of the UK," was all I heard until I caught the word "wave" and for some reason – perhaps because of my location – thought he was talking about some kind of stadium collapse that had happened whilst fans were doing a Mexican Wave.

"Can we speak in a couple of hours?" Dick asked. "I might need to run some things by you but right now nothing's urgent. Just wanted to make sure I could get hold of you."

I agreed that I'd call him back after the game, when I was somewhere a little quieter. I spent the whole game in a state of curiosity. I was itching to find out what had happened and was almost cursing the fact that it had been one of those very rare mornings when we hadn't put on the radio or TV and so I was entirely oblivious of the news. I also found it kind of frustrating that the phone didn't ring again during the 90 minutes of footy. Rotherham won 1–0 but with these thoughts on my mind, I couldn't really appreciate it.

I rang Dick as soon as we were in the car and on the way home. There had been a tsunami involving hundreds of thousands of people in East Asia. I felt the first prickling of fear and adrenaline as Dick explained UK nationals were undoubtedly involved.

"Things are moving fast," Dick said. "This is now a formal request for you to assist. We already have over 600 Grade 1 missing person reports of UK Nationals from all across South East Asia. This could soon be thousands."

"Maybe I would be best placed as your advisor initially?"

Dick was based at Hendon, as was the Casualty Bureau, which had by now opened and had taken thousands of calls and produced hundreds of Grade 1 missing person reports – Grade 1 meaning that the persons reported missing by friends and relatives in the UK were highly likely to have been involved in the Tsunami in that the families or friends had been able to provide accurate information about their location at the time of the disaster. Of course, one of the major factors that had already become apparent was that this incident was not confined to one location; it was geographically spread across thousands of miles. We were receiving calls about people missing in the Maldives, in Sri Lanka, in Thailand, all across South East Asia.

I was facing a totally new scenario in terms of my work in DVI, a scenario in which all kinds of 'trap doors' were hidden but – more importantly – this was a chance for lots of learning. I'd never expected to have to deal with anything on this scale. Forcing down doubts about my abilities and confidence, I called the London Resilience Team, formed to develop a Mass Fatality Plan following 9/11.

"Bodies of some suspected UK nationals are already being flown to Heathrow," I was told. "They're going to Fulham mortuary. We need you there to start with."

I put Sky News on as soon as I got home. As many cops will tell you, Sky News is one of the best briefing tools you can hope for during disasters. Although information was still coming in, camera teams were already giving us a good idea about just how massive the tsunami had been. My phone had gone quiet, and I became so conscious of this that it almost became deafening, and the more I thought about it, the worse it became. I kept checking it to make sure I hadn't missed any calls. I wanted to find out what was happening, yet I knew it would be chaos in London right now, that the Foreign and Commonwealth Office would be taking a hammering and that I should simply sit tight and wait for them to get a grip. After all, it was Boxing Day. People were being recalled from family gatherings across the UK.

I rang Dick Woodman, on the hour every hour but his phone was busy every time. And so I waited. My mental cogs began to turn. Those familiar feelings rose to the surface again, pricking my skin, the ones that questioned my personal limitations, the ones that questioned and tried to shake my confidence and the ones that placed massive expectations upon me. At some point the call would come and I would be expected to tell people what needed to be done. I was scared.

Where the hell do we start with this one? We would be dealing with multiple scenes abroad and with victims being returned to the UK from various locations. I reasoned that the majority of the deceased would be intact, at least at this early stage. So, considering the DVI process, I wondered whether our teams would be able to work abroad and whether or not we would actually be invited. As far as DVI goes, no nation can simply send officers abroad to carry out the process unless the affected country invites you in to do so, even if your own nationals are involved. And then of course, approaches to DVI varied greatly, with some countries not acknowledging it at all while others 'dabble' in the process but aren't particularly thorough.

As it became clear that tens of thousands of people had died, an unimaginable figure, making it difficult to fully understand how the process of DVI would cope in such extraordinary circumstances in a land reeling from the sheer physical destruction the tsunami had wrought. If we were invited to try to identify and retrieve UK victims, what conditions would our DVI teams be working under? There would be little infrastructure amongst the destruction. From fresh water to shelter, all had been destroyed by the killer wave.

Following the 9/11 attacks, plans had been put in place for the UK in the case of extraordinary circumstances. I had worked with Kevin Gordon, seconded from the British Transport Police to the London Resilience Team to develop what came to be called a Mass Fatality Plan (MFP). Kevin and I worked very closely together for a number of years with him tapping into my knowledge and experience of setting up and operating Emergency Mortuaries as the MFP included Emergency Mortuary provisions for the Greater London area and within this, the mortuary at Fulham Hospital (being near to both Heathrow and Gatwick) had been nominated as the receiving and examination mortuary for UK Nationals who died in mass fatality incidents overseas. DVI teams were to work there to authenticate or establish the identity of the victims to ensure that no mistakes were made in repatriating the deceased with their family; it was a necessary quality assurance.

At this time the Coroners' Act (1988) only gave Coroners jurisdiction when a body physically lay within their area and because of this Alison Thompson, who was then Coroner for

London West, was appointed as Coroner for all repatriated Tsunami victims. This was because London West falls within the jurisdiction of Heathrow and all bodies from the Tsunami landed there initially. Clearly not all of the victims lived within that jurisdiction as they were from all over the UK but it was agreed that she would preside over them all on behalf of all Coroners. Alison had experienced the repatriation of British victims following the bombings in Bali in 2002, which killed 202 people, 27 of whom were British.

With all of this in mind, I knew now that I would be best deployed to the Mortuary at Fulham Hospital to work with the Police Mortuary team there. It seemed to make sense that we would have a better chance of doing the best job that we could once the bodies were back in England.

Day became night and still my phone did not ring. I went to bed none the wiser. After a restless night of phone checking I got up and prepared myself for deployment. I was going to wait for the order, I wasn't about to self-deploy as that's not what it's all about; there's no immediate rush with DVI. But by God I was itching to do something and it was painful waiting. It wasn't until the following afternoon, 24hours after first hearing about the disaster that I was contacted again, this time by Chief Superintendent Nick Bracken from the Met, who'd been the SIO for the Selby rail crash. Nick, a member of MDAT, was going to take over the role of SIM for the Tsunami victims returning to the mortuary at Fulham. Nick told me that the Met had sent some officers out to some of the main locations affected not as DVI teams, but as eyes and ears to report back on what was happening. They'd also sent some non-SIM trained senior officers to various places across Asia to link in with and update Nick. The Police National Information and Co-ordination Centre (PNICC, now the National Police Co-ordination Centre or NPoCC) was busy co-ordinating the overall police response nationally, drawing Police DVI resources from all over the country to be ready for deployments.

"I need you to join us for meeting of MDAT at 7pm tomorrow evening at New Scotland Yard," Nick said.

Relieved to be deployed at last, I packed about ten days' worth of clothes and supplies, said my goodbyes to Karon and the family. At this point I really didn't know where I would be going or when I would be back.

As expected, the meeting saw me tasked with advising the police mortuary team at Fulham. I was told that DCI Graham McNulty had been appointed as the Police Silver Commander of the mortuary and so I would be working closely with both him as Silver and Nick as the SIM.

Graham had also been on the SIM course that I had delivered earlier in December. Part of the training programme involved role-play during which, on this particular occasion, Graham was role-playing the SIM and I was playing a Detective Inspector totally ignorant of DVI procedures, the idea being that my lack of knowledge should tease some direction out of Graham as SIM. During the role-play I tied Graham up in knots in front of his colleagues at which point he suddenly snapped and said, quite brilliantly, I felt: "Look Inspector, don't give me the fucking labour pains, just give me the baby!"

I couldn't stop laughing after that and when I could finally string a sentence together over a pint in the bar I told Graham – whom I rated very highly – that one day he might need me. Well, that day had arrived, and our previous encounter stood us in good stead. We couldn't have had a better team.

The meeting confirmed that there were now, officially, about 500 confirmed Grade 1 missing and that the first bodies were due to arrive back the following day, which was when we would begin the DVI process. The idea of processing five hundred people as quickly and as thoroughly as possible was enough to make my mind boggle but I was confident that I could keep things in perspective.

The Met had booked thirty rooms at the Jury's Inn, which was across the road from the mortuary. The rooms were mainly taken by cops from the DVI teams, who were coming from all over the country and by radiographers including Jacquie Vallis whom I'd met on the lecturing circuit, and whose specialism was in forensic radiography for mass fatality incidents. Jacquie was one of the few people truly qualified for this incredibly technical role and I was massively reassured that she would be with us.

The morning began with the news that nine bodies were on the runway at Heathrow ready to be transported to Fulham. They had come from The Maldives, Thailand and Sri Lanka. I was also told that there was only one forensic pathologist available, this being Dr. Rob Chapman based at Fulham. Fortunately Rob was one of the most experienced forensic pathologists in the country – he had performed Princess Diana's autopsy.

Fulham mortuary was meanwhile undergoing a huge transformation, with enhancements including a reception and body storage area for up to seventy bodies. At that time I wasn't sure whether this would be enough or way too much. The Mortuary Facilities Manager at Fulham was a guy called Dave. This was his mortuary which he managed on a day-to-day basis and overnight he had seen it turned into one big 'crime scene', inundated with cops but he was fantastic. He managed to make us feel as though we weren't intruding, even though we'd just turned his world on its head, and made sure that we got everything we needed, despite the massive disruption.

As a kind of ad-hoc mortuary attendant, I was always respectful of the premises I was working in and of the people who were accommodating us, after all, I was a visitor – some may have preferred 'intruder' – who had just stepped into the middle of their 'home'.

I briefed Dave and his staff on the DVI process as they were now going to be part of this much bigger and alien team of DVI personnel. A team of thirty Police Mortuary Officers from the Met that I had trained in 2003 along with a Detective Inspector who was the Police Mortuary Manager, had been deployed as the first teams. The Coroner's Court was right next door to the mortuary, so Identification Commissions could be held there fairly quickly.

As with every operation such as this, we needed to devise standard operating procedures before we could start the work. Although in mass fatality procedures the mortuary work generally involves several areas of examination to obtain evidence to support the identification and to establish a medical cause of death, each incident is different. Therefore, attention has to be paid to obtaining primary identification by the best means possible, given the state and nature of the victims. With that in mind I, along with the Coroner, Nick Bracken and other personnel, had to set about devising the policy, specific to this incident and these victims, before any caskets were opened. I had considered a couple of potential challenges already concerning the identification process. Many of the victims had died in beachwear only, meaning that there would be very few personal items to assist with establishing or confirming identity. So, we developed the policy to focus on the scientific factors of DNA, odontology and fingerprints as primary sources of identification. The name on the casket would be used for intelligence only. The bodies would be searched and stripped with all personal effects being recorded. After this the odontologist would examine teeth and look for comparisons on dental records. As mentioned previously, odontology can confirm identity with 100% accuracy and as such, mitigate the need for further examination. If dental records of the missing were not yet available for comparison, we would move on to fingerprints.

Because we were aware of the potential nature of disruption to the bodies in terms of putrefaction, especially as time went on between recovery overseas and the body being returned, we knew that we had to be thorough in terms of DNA samples and so sought advice from the local forensic science laboratories. They concluded that the best DNA options, in order of use, until identity was established, were:

1. Buccal swabs, to be collected from cheek cells inside the mouth – the least invasive way of collecting DNA.
2. Hair roots
3. The extraction of a cubic centimetre of pink tissue muscle from the thigh area
4. The extraction of two teeth to be ground down
5. The extraction of 8–10 cm of rib or similar length of femur bone.

A few minor issues were thrown up during our discussions. Nick wanted the mortuary teams to do the reconciliations (i.e., the matching of our post-mortem data with the ante-mortem data collected) whereas I wanted – and still believe – that police officers who have had nothing whatsoever to do with any of the other DVI mortuary processes should complete the matching. This avoids any preconceptions regarding identification and mitigates any chance of assumption. I would sooner work from nothing than have any risk of making a body 'fit' what we have in terms of data. I lost that battle on this occasion, but the important thing was that we had developed a thorough policy that covered all eventualities – or so we thought. And so, briefing concluded, facilities ready, we were ready for the first body.

FIFTEEN

THE SHOCK OF THE REAL

I have to admit, I'm a control freak when it comes to work. I don't mean to usurp, I just like to be bang on and get everything just right. This led me to take over a bit at Fulham. The DI, bless him, stood back and basically let me get on with managing the wet side of the operation. The cops were justifiably concerned about the Interpol forms and were generally a bit wary of what they were going to be facing. So together with the Rob, the Forensic Pathologist, I decided to lead the strip-and-search of the first victim, providing the DVI team with a kind of 'master-class' by doing what I train on the courses but with a real body. This, I hoped, would ease us all into the process.

To comply with International Freight Legislation and health and safety in terms of bodily fluids, the bodies were returned cocooned in a sealed zinc case, which was then placed into a coffin. We were unaware of this fact – such was my inexperience in dealing with repatriated victims – and so when we unscrewed the first coffin lid, we were somewhat surprised to be confronted with a sealed metallic box and no way of opening it.

We were rescued by chief mumper Kevin Gordon, who'd taken on the role as the Met's Resource Manager for Fulham. He'd already proved himself as a dedicated and ridiculously resourceful man, solving any issue we had and finding any tool we required – and this was no exception. Within minutes Kevin had sourced an angle grinder. Unfortunately, although there were some DIY heroes among us, no-one had used an angle grinder before, so it took a while before, sparks flying (we were dressed in plastic aprons – risk assessment had gone out the window by this point), the coffin lid was finally cut free.

As the lid was lifted off I didn't see a body at first and thought perhaps we'd just opened an empty coffin. But as it was fully removed, a truly unexpected sight was revealed: a three-month-old baby. We were totally unprepared for this and I froze, struggling to hold my nerve, and then to hold back the tears.

An audience of thirty cops – all similarly psychologically stunned – were waiting for me to do something. I cleared my throat and started my commentary, recording the details of clothing and personal effects. My voice was quavering and I began to sweat as I struggled to maintain my swan on the lake routine – graceful on top, paddling like mad below.

For once, I was grateful that the officers were unsure about the complex Interpol forms. Their questions made a welcome distraction and helped keep me professional. Our policy fell at the first hurdle: there were no teeth, no hair, only fingerprints – but we had nothing to compare them with. That would mean invasive means to extract DNA, which was the last thing any of us wanted. So I spoke with the Coroner who was able to find out about the circumstances of the death. The baby had died in his father's arms. The family, who'd last seen the baby with the undertaker just before they'd flown back, had described the clothing he'd been wearing at the time, which was fairly unique. They also described a teddy bear and a book that had been placed in the casket with their baby. The Coroner, thankfully and sensibly, accepted these corroborative facts and the parents' later viewing of the body as confirmation of identification, meaning that we didn't have to go to scientific means. Nevertheless, this was without doubt one of the most moving and harrowing experiences of my entire life.

But there was no time to dwell or process. Each casket opened was nothing like I had ever seen or dealt with before. By now I was used to massive disruption to bodies on an unimaginable scale for most people. But this... The bodies, although intact, were deeply putrefied. They had died in salt water and had been recovered in temperatures of between 35–40 degrees centigrade. It was unlikely that they had been stored at the correct temperature – four degrees centigrade for up to the first 28 days then a body should go into deep freeze of -15 to -20 degrees centigrade. Hence, they were unrecognisable. I had lived with the stench of death in my nostrils for years but had never experienced anything like this. It was so powerful that the air around the whole of Chelsea Quays was taken over by the rancid, putrid, smell. The only way to cope was to apply my old method: "Just drink it in lad – get it in your nostrils." Some police officers used Vicks Vaporub but this has the opposite of the desired effect, as it just opens up the nasal passages so they take in more of the smell with greater effectiveness.

A complicating factor that made the smell worse was that the bodies had been embalmed; which is where any remaining human bodily fluids are removed and replaced with embalming fluids. In ordinary circumstances this can help to preserve the body, especially during transportation from overseas. In the UK, the concentration of formaldehyde has a professional limit of 5% and the normal formula is one pint of fluid per stone of the body weight plus one pint over. The bodies that we received at Fulham were literally swimming in this incredibly pungent fluid. After the initial, appalling shock, I acclimatised. But the administration staff on the dry side really struggled. They all walked around with handkerchiefs permanently fixed around their noses, wondering how the hell we were hacking it being so close to the smell.

We quickly realised that the options of root hair and buccal swabs were non-starters due to the post-mortem condition of the victims, so once again our protocol proved somewhat ineffective and we had to rely on DNA from the pink tissue, fortunately, we didn't have to get more invasive than this.

Police Family Liaison Officers had been deployed almost immediately to start harvesting the ante-mortem data, including dental records, many of which arrived at the mortuary before the body. Ante and post-mortem data are usually stored separately until the reconciliation process begins, however these were exceptional circumstances and we needed a hasty response. The ante-mortem data was not referred to until the post- mortem and DVI had taken place but having, for example, dental records available as soon as the odontologist required them made the whole process that much quicker, The odontologist at Fulham was Freddie Martin, a great bloke and a seasoned professional who was one of the founder members of the Centre for International Forensic Assistance.

All nine bodies had gone through the DVI process by the afternoon of the next day (December 30) and all had been successfully identified. We soon got into a general routine of working 8am – 6pm as more bodies continued to arrive.

After two or three days, I developed the mother of all headaches. I kept it to myself, wanting not to seem like I was weak or angling for a break. But then others began to get similar symptoms, so we called in the Health and Safety Executive who found that the concentration level of the embalming fluid was 13%, almost triple what was considered acceptable. They threatened to close the mortuary down but we persuaded them to accept a control measure. Once again Chief Mumper Kevin Gordon came up with the goods and obtained five air extractors, each about one-metre square, placed at strategic points in the mortuary. To each was attached a large hose about nine inches in diameter and with length cut to make sure that the fumes were pumped outside – a bit like how a tumble drier with an outlet vent would be plumbed in. These effectively cured the problem for us but of course, pumped more noxious, pungent smells into the air of the Chelsea Quays, much to the dissatisfaction of many of the residents who had spent millions on their luxury pads.

There was very little delay between the bodies returning, going through the DVI process and Commissions being held. In the first few days I literally finished in the mortuary, showered down, met Graham McNulty and went into the Coroner's Court. I narrated the findings as the Coroner's secretary took notes for audit and evidential purposes. She seemed a nice young lady and one evening she tapped me on the shoulder after I had just arrived and whispered if I would mind staying behind for a few moments after the Commission. When the hearing was over, I lingered as requested and the secretary approached. She said, in a low voice: "You're a lovely man but every time you leave this room you leave a smell." I was assured it was nothing personal; I was just carrying the smell of that mortuary, not realising how much it was sticking to my body, in my hair and in my pores. I took more showers and scrubbed harder and that seemed to do the job.

The Met really went to town with this operation. Ingredients were being thrown up to the bosses and they seemed happy enough to put them all into the cake. And rightly so to be fair; no one was going too far in terms of resource-demands; we were just doing a difficult and complex job. Because it was so tough going, I joked to the team one day that a masseuse should be available to help us to relax and ease away our aches. I was genuinely joking but someone passed it on and the Met went and hired one.

I was made co-ordinator and immediately found myself inundated with requests for treatments. For some reason everyone wanted to be first (I think the word masseuse, mentioned to a group of middle-aged men still conjures up images of a beautiful 25-year-old Swedish woman) so we drew straws. The first returned from his massage with a great big smile on his face.

"So what was she like then? Was it any good?" everyone asked, almost at once.

"Yeah, very therapeutic... but he's not as fit as I thought she'd be!"

There was less of a rush after this.

After the first few days we became significantly underworked. My motivation was replaced by a kind of professional boredom as I realised that I had probably done all that I could at Fulham, within that short space of time. I appreciate that this may sound pretty unbelievable due to the number of missing persons reported from the UK and the fact that there were reports of in excess of 250,000 deaths. Initially, bodies had been repatriated without any formal procedures taking place in the countries where the person had died. This meant that we had no way of being sure that those deceased that had been flown home to the UK, were in fact British, or the name on the casket matched that of the victim inside. It is impossible, even with victims intact and, visually identifiable to establish the nationality of a deceased person, without resorting to more in depth scientific examinations. Merely accepting spurious visual identification at the scene of an incident is not reliable for the standards required in the UK, hence our rationale for utilising scientific processes. In relatively quick time, the scale of this operation had been appreciated in the affected foreign countries, and they had instigated the deployment of international DVI teams to those areas which meant that more formal examination procedures were put in place to try to establish identification in that country, before any further victims were repatriated to their supposed country of origin. With that acceptance and introduction of similar processes to ours, came a delay in the repatriation process. The effect was a slower turnover for us in Fulham but a realisation that similar work was being carried out abroad which would increase the chances of accuracy for identification when the victim, was eventually returned to the UK via the Fulham mortuary.

Soon, we were receiving only one or two bodies per day. New Year's Eve was slow in terms of process, although the overall mood was good as people were going home that night to their families. I was supposed to be hosting a New Year's party up North but I ended up staying in Fulham, alone, a real Billy-no-mates. I got quite self-pitying about it at one point, probably made worse due to a couple of whiskeys. I thought that if I was going to be away from home I really ought to be in the thick of it. But New Year's Day was another day. I walked into that mortuary re-focused and ready to fire on maximum revs. Even though we were not working to full capacity, the adrenalin was always there whilst waiting for the next process to begin.

I managed to get home for a couple of days during the first week in January. Having your foot on full throttle for a sustained time does wear you out, so I was ready for the break. Upon my return the dilemma remained; the teams at Fulham did not have enough to do but the quality assurance and control in the UK was definitely needed before the victims were repatriated to their loved ones. The Coroner was keen to facilitate Fulham mortuary getting back to 'normal' work so we began to discuss other ways to do this, negating the need for double identification processes – one, in some form, occurring in the country where the person had died and one again at Fulham – whilst appreciating the political difficulties of our own teams completing the DVI process in someone else's country. So, the Coroner and Nick Bracken went out to Thailand to see if the UK DVI process could in fact be completed to our standards, on site. The difficulty was that we simply couldn't land in a foreign country and dictate our rules and procedures. The knack was diplomacy and the offer of a helping hand and assistance, rather than dictating what we wanted to do. Alison and Nick were the right people to initiate discussions.

I'd talked to a number of people deployed in Asia about the mortuary facilities over there. From what I could gather, the devastation was on such a massive scale that it seemed as though there was little chance of establishing facilities for DVI to be done properly. And still, the deceased victims who were thought to be UK Nationals, like others, had spurious identifications done around the time of death. There seemed to be no continuity out there, a person was generally initially identified wherever they had died, removed from that location, taken to a mortuary, then transferred to an aircraft and returned back without a full audit or tracking of the body. That said, in 21 days we took 27 bodies through the DVI process at Fulham and, incredibly, 25 of those were found to belong to UK Nationals and were indeed who the casket said they were. I was surprised really at what was a very high percentage given the potential and rather large margin for error. But it only takes one mistake to devastate a family.

For the two victims who were found not to be UK Nationals, we completed the post-mortem forms as per the usual process and retained their bodies at Fulham. The evidence obtained (our post mortem data) was then returned to the country from which the bodies were transferred – in other words from where they had died – in anticipation that this would be matched with ante-mortem information at a later time. That indeed did happen. The two victims were later identified, confirmed as being foreign nationals and they were subsequently repatriated to their own countries. This proved to me, although I didn't need any convincing, that the DVI process works. It's about achieving a positive identification on a deceased person but of course in trying to reach that sometimes we discover that the deceased is not the individual we thought they were. Whilst this can be disappointing, it does mean that we are thorough enough to never return a body to a family without knowing that it is definitely their loved one. So, although providing a minor storage problem, we proved via these two cases, that the system worked because our post-mortem data was fed back into the investigation in the country where they died and subsequent matches were made resulting in positive identifications. In such circumstances, this clearly does not happen overnight. The secret is patience, diligence and tenacity. We can usually find plenty of primary and secondary identification evidence in the post-mortem examination during DVI but in the absence of ante-mortem data, identification cannot be made.

Upon their return, the Coroner and Nick Bracken reported that the Thai Authorities were really keen to continue to get this right and by now 39 countries were already deployed across Asia and were carrying out DVI processes to some degree, where the incidents had happened. Nick was invited back over to work alongside the Thai Police Commander and in effect became the SIM for the whole operation, managing all of the identifications within Thailand. This made our job so much easier and ensured a level of control over identification standards. As a result, the decision was made to start scaling down the mortuary at Fulham, with teams on standby. Gradually, Fulham got back to business as usual, taking in the UK victims along with day-to-day procedures, as and when they were repatriated. A team of DVI officers from the Met were on standby for deployment at the mortuary and quality assurances were carried out to corroborate the identifications, which again had to be subjected to the Identification Commission for Coroner's approval.

On the morning of 14 January I was called in to see Police Commander John Bunn who told me I was going to be deployed to Thailand to assist the mortuary teams out there. My tasks were to provide advice, look at the quality assurance side of things and look at the repatriation process with an ultimate aim of negating any further requirement for Fulham. I knew that the first two tasks in my remit would be no problem but I also knew that the repatriation side would be challenging, as I had never done this while deployed abroad.

Although the Police National Information Co-ordination Centre policy was that a maximum of two weeks should be spent actually working in the mortuary, I was scheduled to be there for nineteen days and would be working with South Wales Police who were the next team due out.

I had never been to Thailand before but oddly enough, Karon and I had booked to go there for a holiday in March that year. I rang Karon to tell her that I was travelling back home that day, for one night only before catching my flight on Friday to Bangkok then on to Phuket. She was extremely supportive and understood that I was the National Advisor on all this, that I had to be completely focused. At the same time, she was clearly worried. Just before I left for my flight she aked me: "Does it not worry you that you're going to a place where disasters happen? There might be another Tsunami."

I made a dismissive "I'll be fine, don't worry," response at the time but I have to admit, she had a point.

I got home by 2pm on the Thursday and was back at New Scotland Yard less than 24hrs later where I joined the man who was leading the South Wales team for a briefing from one of the Met Detective Superintendents, Graham Walker. He told us that the Thais were in command and had a good supporting structure but followed this with a warning about just how horrendous and dangerous the conditions were. Before we knew it we were on our way. As we left, Karon's words came back to me and it hit me that I was going to face something truly awful.

Soon, I was on the plane together with the mortuary manager from South Wales. We were travelling to Thailand three days in advance of his team starting work in order to find our bearings and so we could organise a decent handover. By now I was used to being a big fish in a little pond but I was aware I was going to very much be the little fish in a very big pond. I remained keen to learn as ever, however, and was curious to see whether the other countries who had sent DVI teams out there differed from us in any way.

I've found that the strangest things pre-occupy and concern me when I'm trying to deal with something substantial. Perhaps it's easier to focus on the more insignificant things that you can rationalise and my mind turned to the fact that the UK team didn't have a corporate 'livery'. I worried that we wouldn't 'look' professional even though we were – first impressions and all that. That was my main pre-occupation as the airplane engines hummed quietly through the night and, as I drifted in and out of sleep, my mind flitted between the inconsequential and wondering what exactly I was flying into. Would I be able to cope with the as yet unknown challenges that were about to be thrown my way?

SIXTEEN
230,000

L anding at Bangkok airport twelve hours later, I was surprised
at how awake I felt. This was partly fuelled by adrenalin and
partly fuelled by the warm welcome we received from the
Thai people – regardless of the fact that their country was still
reeling from a major disaster. I quickly grew familiar with the
word 'Sawadee' (the polite way of saying 'hello') in those first
few hours; it was an extraordinary and humbling experience.
After changing planes we flew on to Phuket and as soon as we
stepped out of the airport, the heat hit me like a hot, wet blanket.
It couldn't have been more different from the freezing January air
we had left behind in the UK; I found it intoxicating.

Our hotel, the Laguna Beach was so ornately luxurious that
I felt completely wrong-footed, and struggled to reconcile what I
was there for. The fact that this country had just suffered tremendous devastation simply seemed unreal. The only indication that
things were not as they should be was that there almost no tourists at the hotel which – incredibly – was providing free accommodation to international DVI workers. They just wanted to 'do
their bit' to help which I thought was overwhelmingly generous.
I would soon realise that this is what the Thai people are naturally like. I was receiving a Home Office overseas allowance of US

$125 a day and so it seemed only right to donate the hotel accommodation cost equivalent to the Tsunami disaster fund that was set up for the local people. The majority of my colleagues did likewise. Thailand's main source of income had been eradicated overnight due to an unexpected and unstoppable event. For them to maintain such dignity post-incident, for them to carry on with so much spirit, left an impression that will stay with me for the rest of my life.

It was 9.30pm by the time I'd checked-in. I dumped my bags and headed to the bar for a swift nightcap, joined by the guy from South Wales. We chewed the fat a bit before turning in, having met up with some of the cops who'd been working there over the last few weeks and who I knew, as I'd trained them in DVI. I was really grateful to be able to have this time with them, not only because it helped me to settle in but also because it was important to glean as much information as I could in advance of the tough task ahead.

My brief on departure from the UK was that I would be acting as an advisor to the Inspector who, in this case was the guy leading the South Wales contingent. Apart from attending one of my three-day DVI courses about one year earlier, the Inspector, like the majority of his team had no DVI experience whatsoever. His teams were due to fly out after him a couple of days later so we needed to formulate the handover from the current team and prepare a briefing for the incoming South Wales team. Easier said than done, especially for me, as I found that I had to familiarise myself with the existing working practices and 'fit' into those, in complete contrast to what I had been used to, i.e., being instrumental in devising or at least advising on working practices from the outset.

The next day, after a restless night, it was straight to work. The UK mortuary lead that was currently out there with his team was Kevin Instance, an Inspector from Avon and Somerset Police. He met me at the hotel and together with the South Wales Inspector we made our way to 'Site 1' at Wat Yan Yao. This was about 60km north of Khow Llak on the South West coast of the Peninsula and a highly popular tourist area that had suffered thousands of fatalities. It was around a two-hour drive from where we were staying.

Site 1: the somewhat undignified name given to the area now designated as a mortuary. It was actually a Buddhist temple, the grounds of which seemed to be about the size of a football pitch. It looked very much like a cemetery from the outside with short walls and metal railings protecting the perimeter. On the surrounding roads stood a large number of street market stalls, staffed by locals, selling all kinds of products, but predominantly locally-produced food. I was a bit shocked at first because they were just on the edge of the mortuary but it made sense. A large number of foreign DVI workers meant some desperately-needed custom. None of the stallholders seemed at all fazed by the horrors that lay only a few yards away.

As we walked towards the entrance, Kevin told me that this was a shared site, with the Thais occupying half of the space. They had permitted foreign DVI teams to operate in their country and to share this designated area on the understanding that they (the Thais) examined and dealt with their deceased and that the 'farang' (foreigners) would in turn, be dealt with by their own people. My immediate thought echoed one that I had back in the UK; how can one determine the nationality of a deceased person before any examination has taken place, particularly after putrefaction has set in and an aesthetic assessment is impossible? Surely that's what DVI is all about, so how were they getting past this crucial first step? I was going to have to wait a while before I could even try and find out. The Thais were about re-locate their mortuary facility to another Buddhist Temple area about ten minutes down the road. This was to be called Site 1a and we, as 'farang' would not be encouraged to go there unless exceptional circumstances dictated that we needed to. This was in order to respect the Thais' privacy.

The entrance to Site 1 distracted me considerably from Kevin's briefing. Before me was an ornate red, gold and blue pointed archway built in traditional Thai style. Beyond this was an even more ornate stone temple about sixty feet tall, also red, gold and blue. As we entered I noticed the sun shelters that had been erected at various locations in the grounds. They looked like gazebos with no sides. There were tents, porta cabins and other temporary structures serving as makeshift body storage units and mortuary facilities. My initial impression was that there seemed no semblance of organisation. There was no obvious process route evident and it all seemed disjointed, there was no flow. That said, of course I appreciated that the circumstances and the environment being worked in was extreme.

There were already a number of nations working within Site 1. Kevin took us to the mobile incident room from which the overall co-ordination was being done. It was full of Police Commanders from the Australian and New Zealand teams, who I discovered, were taking the lead. They had a corporate identity with smart uniforms and a DVI insignia so they really looked as if they knew what they were doing.

Site 1 was next to a river that emptied into the Andaman Sea approximately two kilometres away. Along the riverbanks stood metal reefers, one after another. They looked like freight containers but I knew that inside each lay dozens of victims. They had lain in those unrefrigerated metal boxes in incredible heat for days on end. As we approached, I tried to prepare, to get my head around the idea of exactly how unpleasant opening the reefers up might be. I started to brace myself. I kind of knew what to expect but was still unsure. As the door was opened the thick stench poured out over me. Blinking though the smell, I could see dozens of bodies literally piled up on top of one another. We were told that police officers had to wear BA (breathing apparatus) each time they came to collect a body. As the door closed I realised that I would be working with this every day but strangely, I already knew I would be ok with that.

Dogs, attracted by the smell, were running freely around the Site. I thought that Fulham was bad but this... You honestly can't begin to imagine unless you have had the misfortune to come into contact with dozens of rotting corpses. Think of a warehouse with a temperature of 35 degrees that contains putrefied meat that has been there for days, even weeks with no refrigeration, mixed in with rotting vegetables and the worst sweaty socks that you have ever smelt in your life and you are maybe halfway there. Add to this an overriding stench of a huge lake containing nothing but raw sewerage and you might get a little bit closer. You would think that it would be less concentrated as it was in the open air, but by God, it took some getting used to.

The conditions at Site 1 were pretty appalling and miles away from being anything like clinical. There weren't any showers but local Thais were providing 24hr catering to the Site and the Thai Army were doing all of the lifting and shifting of the bodies between storage and mortuary so there were some 'luxuries'. Kevin advised me that 'Site 2' was still under construction. The aim for Site 2 was that it would be 'more conventional' in terms of facilities and it was being purposefully built for foreign DVI teams to work in. The Thais termed it a 'field hospital', which seemed a bit odd to me, as no victims were ever going to be leaving there cured. Site 2 was to be at Mai Khao, still on the island of Phuket and about 150 kilometres south of Site 1. It was very close to Phuket airport and as such, more convenient for us, as our hotel was less than a thirty-minute drive away. A Norwegian company, 'Normica', was going to provide the body storage and mortuary facilities, which would consist of three examination pods and there would also be administration blocks, catering and welfare amenities. The plan was to develop a 'mortuary village'. Once this had been completed all 'farang' would be transported to Site 2.

After visiting Site 1 we commenced the long return journey to our base in Phuket. It was during this journey that Site 1a was pointed out to me. It looked similar to Site 1 from the outside but the railings had been covered with tarpaulin sheets to maintain a degree of privacy. As we drove past the open entrance I stretched my neck to try to catch a glimpse through the gap. I saw a number of the metal reefers lined up side by side, forming a second but less penetrative boundary. I couldn't help but be intrigued as to what was going on beyond those storage containers. What might the Thais be doing that was different to our examination processes? I concluded that I shouldn't search for an answer; they just required and deserved the privacy to deal with their dead in their own way.

What I had seen at Wat Yan Yao left me pre-occupied. I could see that it would benefit from a bit of order in terms of the process flow there and I thought this could be sorted relatively easily. The only thing that really bothered me was the travelling there and back every day. But I had had a taster and now I was anxious to get stuck in and start work. Over the next couple of days the Detective Inspector from South Wales and I started to think about what we needed to tell his team. He relied upon on me to provide adequate tools for his briefings, which I didn't mind one bit. I worked hard bringing him up to speed and helping him to get a full grasp of the essentials so that by the time that his team had arrived, settled and were due to be deployed, he was prepared enough to give a good briefing and account of what was required.

Initially, about eighteen members of the UK Police contingent were deployed at Site 1, though that was soon to change as within a few days of starting work, Site 2 opened; hence the team was split between the two sites. Although not completely ready, pressures had been mounting for Site 2 to open and start taking all of the 'farang', maybe due to the sheer volume of bodies being taken to Site 1 even with Site 1a operating and maybe due to the fact that the Thais were keen to focus on their own dead and let us process ours. Two separate sites made sense but I still wondered how they could tell Westerners from locals.

I only ended up working at Site 1 for the first 3 days before moving to Site 2, which was a much shorter journey from the Laguna Beach. Those already working there were trying out a new system. There were nine international teams deployed at Site 2 all being co-ordinated by a Mortuary Management Group headed by a guy called Leif. As the UK lead at this Site, I was invited to sit on that Group and because the Site was starting from afresh, I was able to contribute to the discussions regarding how the mortuary should operate. That was really beneficial, particularly as the Chair of the Group was receptive of advice, and was pleased to have someone experienced on hand. After the first meeting we had formulated a method of operations and developed a policy document, written in English – that provided a sound basis for a formal and professional way of working. That said, the utter scale of the task had not yet been fully realised.

For all my previous work in DVI, I had been involved from the beginning right through to the end. This was new territory for me, as I knew I would only be a small chapter in what was going to be an extremely long story. I found this both odd and kind of frustrating but I was determined to do justice to the roles I had been tasked with and at least see them through to some beneficial conclusion.

I arrived for work at Site 2 after the first two pods had been constructed but when there was still no electricity or running water. There were two shifts. The working day was 8am–5pm, or

4pm–midnight but once a body had started to go through the DVI process it had to be completed regardless of any complications or timings shift-wise. The condition of the bodies meant that some disciplines took a long time to conclude, meaning that people involved in others were left hanging, sometimes for hours. We didn't always get the timings right but knew how crucial both thoroughness and accuracy were. Most of the bodies had been given a Thai unique reference number after being recovered from where they died but as I had thought when working at Fulham, there was a massive lack in continuity from scene to mortuary and therefore a massive lack in integrity. As part of our standard operating procedures at Site 2 we decided that we should start from scratch and so everybody brought in to the process, despite having being allocated a Thai body number, was given a new number which included a reference to the site where we had examined the body, i.e., Site 2 = 2 as well as the international dialling code for whichever team had dealt with the whole DVI process for that victim; so all of ours had 44 as part of the new number. We would then issue the body with a new sequential number as it was brought into the examination process. This new number was always cross-referenced with the number originally provided by the Thais, which was always shown on the label. So, for example, the body number would look like this: -2- 44.1225 (Thai 5467). This helped with some of the continuity issues.

My first shift on Site 2 was an evening shift starting at 4pm. We figured that if we could process nine bodies per team per day that would be good going and if all of the international DVI teams worked at that rate up to a hundred bodies per day would have been processed.

I've seen many documentaries on the Tsunami since going to Thailand and one that sticks in my mind was a Horizon programme shown in May 2005 which covered the work that the British DVI teams were doing. A cop was narrating at one point and talking about how primitive the facilities were out there but I noted that he said they had electricity, running water, a canteen and a rest area. I had to smile because for that first and the next few subsequent evening shifts, we had no running water and no electricity. It got dark around 6pm and the carriage of bodies and autopsies were taking place under the beam of a Volvo's headlights! I have to admit that initially it was all a bit of a shambles, only to be expected as we just were not geared up for those conditions. We were trying to do Disaster Victim Identification justice on what was essentially a working building site. The number of slips, trips and falls became almost ridiculous. Health and safety and risk assessments were completely absent. The nearest we came to having Health and Safety acknowledged wasn't even directly connected to the work in the mortuary itself. It was thanks to a coconut. Site 2 was built on an old burial ground surrounded by palm and coconut trees. I couldn't help but notice that coconuts were falling all around us, and we were in the line of fire when we walked to and from work. At the time I didn't know that falling coconuts are the biggest single killer of tourists in the world and we ignored the problem until after about a week, I passed by a parked car with a huge V-shaped dent in its roof, the result of a coconut. So the Mortuary Management Group convened a meeting, to which the Thai site janitor was invited and was asked if he had a solution. Looking extremely chilled, he said that he could cure the problem no worries and that we should be ready with our cameras ready at 2pm that day. Curious, a few of us gathered to see what great technological feat the 'cure' was. At the promised time, a Thai guy pulled up in his truck, got out of the driver's side and in Thai, promptly shouted instructions to a monkey, which was sitting in the pick-up's passenger seat. The monkey got out of the vehicle cab, jumped into the open back and sat on the tailboard, looking all coy as the watching humans started to snap away. The guy placed a lead on the collar of the monkey and then led it off towards one of the offending palm trees. Another command was given whereupon the monkey immediately started to climb and then wrestle off the coconuts one-by-one, dropping them to the ground, only when instructed that it was safe to do so. It was fascinating to watch and unbelievable how effective the remedy actually was. That monkey worked its nuts off for us until one day it attempted to chew through some electric cable and was promptly electrocuted. I was back in the UK when I received this piece of news and I was sorry to hear our hard-working monkey had met such a sudden and traumatic end.

At this time there were no Thai soldiers available to assist at Site 2, so the UK teams were initially responsible for the 'lifting and shifting' – collecting from and logging the bodies as being out of storage, delivering them to the mortuary and once the extraction of post-mortem identification evidence gathering was complete, returning them to where they had come from and logging them back into storage. I'm relieved to say that body storage had improved tremendously at Site 2; small units containing eighteen bodies or larger units containing seventy bodies were used with staging and racking inside which allowed for far more dignity than the deceased being piled up in reefers.

Unlike at Site 1, most of the victims were in body bags here, which was much better in terms of dignity and respect but as there was still no refrigeration and the rate of putrefaction was therefore further accelerated. This was the great irony of this job: the nature of the incident itself was not particularly disruptive to the bodies but was the conditions in which they were stored were; limbs were being separated and all sorts. Again, incredibly when you consider what would put in place today, the things that we were potentially being exposed to were not really considered. We had some routine inoculations just before being deployed and were taking malaria tablets but whether or not they had had time to get into our systems and kick in we did not know. All manner of 'mishaps' were taking place that compromised the health of officers.

One evening, I and a couple of other officers went to collect the next body from storage, which happened to be on the top shelf of the racking. It was enormous and I wondered why on earth such a heavy body had been placed on the top rack. After a bit of shoving to and fro, we guesstimated the weight to be about twenty stone (127kg). We didn't have trolleys and there was no other means of carrying the bodies except via ourselves, and with only a single file corridor within the unit to move in, so I figured that the best way to deal with this one was if two of us bent over, making our backs into a sturdy platform, whilst the other officers gently lowered the body onto us. I duly leaned forward, and braced myself for the weight and together with another officer, formed the platform. The body bag was oh-so carefully lifted off the racking and gently rested onto our backs – at which point it promptly burst. Although I was wearing a tyvek suit, most of the liquid remains went straight down my back. It was like warm soup and the sensation was truly sickening. The guys lifted what was left of the body off me and I ran to the little 'scout' tent that served as a bit of a changing area/first-aid post. I rubbed myself down as best I could with what I found in there – paper towels and some bottled water – before getting back to work. It troubled me and played on my mind for a while not only because of what had happened to the victim but also because of my health. There was no such thing as incident reporting, there were no control measures in place and so it really was ultimately a case of survival. Eventually, much to my relief, some body carts arrived at Site 2. They were very simple in nature – rigid and wooden with two pram-type wheels – but they did the job, just about. Unfortunately, we couldn't get these carts into the reefers, they wouldn't fit, no-way-no-how, and so there was still a bit of delicate manual work, if not as much.

∗ ∗ ∗

Eventually, the UK teams ended up working with Jane, a pathologist from New Zealand, and her pathological technician, Robbie, which was really good for us as it afforded my team the opportunity to gain experience in the full process and get fully involved in what they had been deployed to do. The state of putrefaction dictated that for the fingerprinting process, which was the first point of examination, four officers were needed per victim plus a scribe.

Fingerprints are considered to be – alongside teeth and DNA – to be one of the three primary identifiers. Like DNA and odontology, the usefulness of this identification technique can vary with the disaster and state of the cadavers. For the Asian Tsunami, fingerprinting joined odontology as one of the two most important methods of identification.

The skin has two layers, the epidermis, the outer layer of epithelial scales, and an inner layer of dense connective tissue known as the dermis. Mostly, the skin is stickier on the posterior area of the body but this is reversed on the hands and feet. The outer surface of the skin of the hands and feet is – unlike the skin on the rest of the body – arranged in a series of grooves which are known as furrows and ridges which are supposed to help us grip onto things. Our fingerprints are created by the patterns of these ridges, which – although lying parallel to one another – twist and turn and start and stop in patterns that are unique to each individual. Our fingerprint pattern forms in the foetus and remains the same throughout our lives and beyond death – until decomposition has taken hold. Sweat glands on the summits of each of the ridges cause us to leave latent fingerprints wherever we go.

In terms of the type of pattern about 60 to 65% of the population has loops, 30 to 35% has whorls and around 5% has arches. There are subdivisions within these three broad categories, which give the basis of the ten-point classification system in current usage. As a conclusive identification tool, we've relied on the fingerprint system for over a century. The Fingerprint Bureau at New Scotland Yard was established in July 1901 in the wake of the publication in 1900 of *Classification and Uses of Fingerprints* by Sir Edward Henry.

Fingerprinting was chosen to be the first station as it was quite correctly thought that we needed to secure this vital evidence at an early stage before any more skin tissue was lost as the bodies moved through the mortuary. Exposure to salt water and aggravated storage temperatures meant that the skin of victims was starting to peel off. Fingerprints are quite deep through the various layers of skin but will be lost if sufficient layers of the skin are lost. Despite also being unique, a decision was taken not to obtain footprints as the work involved in obtaining ante-mortem samples to compare them with would have been almost impossible. Everyone leaves fingerprints in their homes, hotels, places they have occupied and some are on criminal records data bases, but footprints are not held as such and to obtain a suspected victim's print from their home or last place of occupancy is not so straightforward, as in the UK at least we rarely walk around in bare feet and if we do, it tends to be on carpeted floors.

Due to the rate of putrefaction of the majority of victims in Thailand, the hands had to be injected to make them swell, and then soaked in boiling water, which enabled the removal of the epidermis from the hand. Following the removal of the skin, it was carefully and delicately rolled onto an officer's finger, which in turn allowed the impression to be rolled across the ink and onto the relevant pad. This process, called de-gloving, provided an opportunity to obtain primary identification evidence with minimum disruption to the victims. If this sounds gruesome, and it is, consider the fact that after the Marchioness Disaster it was revealed that it was standard practice for fingerprint officers to remove the hands of the deceased after a mass fatality incident so they could be sent to the Metropolitan police laboratory for printing. Of the 25 individuals who had their hands removed after the sinking of the Marchioness, only three were identified through the use of fingerprints, the rest of the identifications being achieved through dental records. Some of the hands were nonetheless removed after this positive identification had been made. Finally, in a number of cases the hands were not returned to the body before the body was released to the family. Policy and procedure have long since changed and the Interpol guide to DVI states that during PM examination of bodies it is essential to ensure that only unavoidable changes are made to the bodies. This is recognised in the approach taken by fingerprint experts in the UK today. All officers involved in DVI will do their utmost not to disturb bodies any more than they have to but as far as de-gloving went, back then there was simply no other way. Thanks to technological advances it's now possible to rely on digital photography for fingerprinting in cases like this.

Following the fingerprint process, the body was next stripped and searched, with the police scribe recording all details throughout, including those described by the pathologist. By the time I arrived in Phuket, DNA samples could only be obtained through 5–10cm of bone from the ribcage or 5–10cm of bone from the femur. As previously mentioned the routine order for DNA harvest is buccal swab from the inside of the cheek followed by a root from the hair if identity is unsuccessful from the former. Neither of these methods were suitable due to the condition of the bodies and nor was the next course, which was to take pink deep muscle tissue from the thigh – after one week in storage in that heat there was no tissue left. Thus only intrusive means remained viable; the first for consideration was to extract DNA from the teeth, a task which would have to be carried out by a forensic scientist in a sterile laboratory location. In terms of the process, two untreated teeth would be removed and if a DNA profile was successfully extracted from the first ground-down tooth then the second was not examined and was returned to the body intact. As sterile laboratory facilities were not available to us within Thailand, we relied on samples from the femur/ribcage until the ICMP in Bosnia offered to help and all samples, including teeth, were eventually sent to them for analysis.

Outside of DNA the final part of the process was odontology. X-rays were taken of teeth, before any removals for DNA, to provide a post-mortem dental chart and these were subsequently compared against any ante-mortem dental records that could be obtained. Forensic dentistry has played a major role in identification methods throughout human history; the body of Emperor Nero's battered mistress was identified by her teeth as long ago as AD50. Teeth – the hardest tissue in the human body – are the piece of us that is the most resistant to trauma, decomposition, fire and water immersion. Teeth are therefore of immense value when identifying bodies in the wake of a mass disaster and they have played a key role in the investigations into the Lockerbie air disaster, the London bombings of 2005, and the Dhow boat disaster of 2006, in which 57 people died, after a crowded pleasure boat capsized off the coast of Bahrain. Dental identification can still outplay DNA as a quick, economic and reliable way to identify the deceased, as long as comparable ante-mortem records are available. The teeth also store DNA in the pulp cavity, the innermost layer of the tooth, which is more or less sealed and so can help in cases where DNA is required from a body, which might be extensively damaged and/or contaminated. Apart from identification, teeth can also be used as a means to determine someone's age.

A forensic dentist will depend on family liaison officers to contact the dental practitioners of the missing, as well as dental clinics, specialists, doctors and hospitals. Items such as dentures, toothbrushes (for DNA) and mouth guards can all be used in the identification process. It is also helpful to have recent photographs of the person smiling and/or showing their teeth. Occasionally it's necessary for the forensic dentist to contact the missing person's dentist personally to clarify certain aspects of their dental history.

In the dental section, dentists usually work in teams of two; one "clean," doing the recording and assisting and one "dirty," undertaking the actual examination. Photographs are taken of the facial structures, both frontal and profile. The mandible (jaw) is exposed and photographs are taken. Teeth are cleaned and any loose teeth are repositioned. The teeth are photographed, as are any dentures, tongue piercings, braces and any other relevant material. X-rays are taken of all of the teeth, in accordance with the dental protocol, which is followed by a detailed full mouth examination and charting. Both dentists will sign the forms. The extraction of a tooth, usually a large molar, is made for DNA analysis. At the completion of the examination, the replacement of any tissue, dentures, bridges etc., is performed to restore the person's dignified appearance.

The post-mortem details were then entered into a computer-matching program. Computers saved a great deal of time in Thailand, considering the thousands of bodies awaiting identification. But, as with any computer program, its success depends upon the quantity and particularly the quality of the input information. Suggested matches between AM and PM information identified by the programme must then be examined in detail and any discrepancies must be explained before a tentative match can be accepted.

Radiographs – essential for finding hidden dentistry – are also taken, which might reveal crowns, root fillings, route abscesses, etc., which might have gone unseen in the visual mouth examination.

Superimposition of AM and PM radiographs have often been used successfully to confirm comparisons.

An identification is categorised in one of five ways:

1. Established (beyond doubt)
2. Probable (very likely)
3. Possible (no discrepancies but insufficient unique information to confirm identity beyond doubt)
4. Excluded (the information precludes a match)
5. Insufficient information comfortably to establish any of the above conclusions.

Probable and possible matches are useful in that they can be used to focus other disciplines such as fingerprints and DNA. With an established identification the AM and PM hardcopies are checked, compared again and, if all is in order, the files are sent to the identification commission for final approval of identification.

As far as the tsunami was concerned, a policy decision had been made that the cause of death for all victims was drowning and so during the autopsies the pathologists were looking primarily for any clues that might help with identification; any medical conditions, prosthetics, whether a pacemaker had been fitted, signs of operations such as appendectomy or gall bladder removal; anything that may assist. It was extremely busy and photographs were taken throughout, which was absolutely correct for evidential purposes but something that I was extremely uneasy with was the amount of video-recording and 'extra' photography that seemed to be taking place. I've never seen so much.

This would be fine if it was being taken for training purposes, but I wasn't always convinced that this was the case.

Of course, because this was an international incident our officers were using the Interpol mortuary forms. Although I remained opposed to them in their current format, I concede that they did the job for us in Thailand. Because the process was much slower due to the condition of the victims, the forms actually didn't slow it down any further. It was my job to oversee the whole process and quality-check all of the paperwork to ensure that every form had been completed with accuracy and as fully as possible. Once I was satisfied, the forms were sent to the Incident Management Centre (IMC) building in Phuket. This was a building normally occupied by the Telecommunications of Thailand Company but was given over to provide the command centre for this disaster. It was there that all the matching with ante-mortem data received took place, by other specialist staff not involved in the mortuary examination process. As I mentioned previously, it makes sense to me to have independent people unconnected to either the ante-mortem harvest or post-mortem examination to carry out the comparisons. This part of the identification process, the 'reconciliation', is the final stage before the evidence is submitted to the Identification Commissions, which were also held in the IMC building. As you can imagine, it was a really difficult and traumatic process but the aim remained clear and as always, it kept me and others going, as we knew that accurate compilation of post-mortem data would help to correctly identify UK citizens allowing their bodies to be repatriated back home to their families.

One week into my deployment in Thailand I had to go back to Site 1. Conditions still weren't brilliant but there did at least seem to be more order to the process. I met a team of anthropologists who had been drafted in and who were working alongside other specialists carrying out examinations to try to determine which deceased victims were 'farang' and which were South East Asian and therefore to be delivered to Site 1a. Although not the purpose for my visit, I learned how you can tell which body should go to which site. Whilst not ultra-scientific, there were considerations around simple things such as the type of tattoo a victim had, which often in itself gave a good indication. But it mainly comes down to bone structure. The shape of the upper and lower jaw bones provided a good clue as South East Asians have a different configuration in their upper jaw to Westerners; in South East Asians at the back of the head where the spine meets the skull bone the bone is flat, in Westerners it is raised; measurements from hip bone to ankle bone via the femur, fibula and tibia in Westerners it is 60% femur and 40% fibula and tibia whereas in South East Asians it is a 50–50% proportion. This was a quick and effective way of distinguishing locals from 'farang'. The anthropologists worked on somewhere in the region of 8,000 bodies at Phuket and seldom got a body placing wrong.

Foreign teams that had remained working at Site 1 very rarely went near or into Site 1a in order to afford the Thais upmost privacy and respect. But events transpired that made it necessary for me to visit Site 1a, as we thought that a teenage UK National who was aesthetically similar to a Thai might have been taken there instead of Site 2. As we had been advised that under normal circumstances we shouldn't go to Site 1a, we thought it prudent ask for permission via the UK Senior Identification Manager to visit Site 1a. We soon got the nod. I was with Kevin Instance and two other UK DVI team members when we entered the site and were met by a Hawaiian pathologist called Steve Wilson who was dressed in a lemon-coloured tyvek suit.

"You can check, no problem," he told us. I asked Steve how he had ended up at Site 1a. "I just turned up at the gate and they invited me in," he replied with a smile.

We were required to gown-up with protective suits and wellingtons before we entered the site beyond the storage units, which was an open area, again about the size of a football pitch. As we approached, the view was shocking. There were around two hundred bodies lying head-to-toe, row-upon-row, one after another. No body bag. No shroud. It seems strange to say this bearing in mind what I had been dealing with over the previous week, but it was at this moment, surveying all of those dead people, that the magnitude of the incident really hit me. To be confronted with that number of deceased in one place, all within view, it was truly horrific. And this was just a very small proportion of the many thousands of victims yet to be processed. That sight has remained with me ever since and occasionally appears in my dreams.

It was important for me to find the missing boy not only because it was a high-profile case but also because it was right that he should be at Site 2 so that correct identification and repatriation could take place. We spent a long time looking and at one point I thought we'd found him until the odontology proved me wrong. I was extremely disappointed. I don't like to 'fail' at anything but his body was eventually found in April, his identity confirmed via ante-mortem dental records, and his family were at last given closure.

So far in my deployment I had provided advice and guidance in the mortuary, ensured quality control, good audits and checks of the Interpol Forms being completed by the UK teams and as per my original tasking, I was now asked to concentrate on devising a policy for the repatriation process. It was advantageous to have operated the 'receiving' mortuary at Fulham, as I knew that all bodies being repatriated from abroad still had to go through a duplicate examination in London to corroborate the findings of any Identification Commission in either Thailand or from Sri Lanka. This 'belt and braces' approach was ideal but now that UK

DVI teams were operating abroad, albeit under the direction and rules of the host country, the need to duplicate the examination at Fulham seemed unnecessary. Besides, the Fulham mortuary had to be freed up to go back to business as usual so could not remain dedicated to Tsunami victim examinations indefinitely.

I spoke with Alison Thompson in Fulham and we agreed that, whatever we did we should not upset or insult the Thais by questioning their standards of investigation. The current process was that after hearing reconciliation evidence, the Thai Identification Commission would declare identification proved and would issue a release and death certificate. The Foreign and Commonwealth Office had representatives in Phuket who basically acted as agents for the families. They had agreed to fly home, or to use the correct term, repatriate UK victims, at Governmental expense, but the wishes of the families were always taken into account. A local undertaker would collect the deceased from the Site 2 mortuary and bring that victim to a designated repatriation site, which was several miles away on the outskirts of Phuket town. Accompanying the body was the previously mentioned paperwork together with a report of the findings of the Identification Commission and reasons for declaring identification proved. I have to say that the standard of DVI, in my opinion was excellent, but of course the UK Coroner needs to be satisfied that this identification has been achieved as per Coroner's Act standards in England and Wales. It simply would not have been right to undertake a further full examination at the repatriation site to confirm identification, but if any mistakes in the process had been made thus far, then equally it made sense to discover these before the body was repatriated 7,000 miles to the UK. We decided that the most sensible way to progress would be for us to have any ante-mortem descriptions and where accessible, ante mortem dental records to hand as the victims were brought to the repatriation site. Under scenes of crime conditions, i.e. photography at every stage, the body was re-examined superficially for marks, scars, tattoos, malformations, amputations, anything which the family had stated we would find externally on their loved one. I carried out at least six examinations under this policy – which as with all good practice had to be slightly amended as we undertook each examination – and was amazed how many corroborating features we found. Of course with a post-mortem dental examination and comparing ante-mortem dental records, we knew unquestionably that we had the right body.

No further examinations took place and our findings were recorded contemporaneously. Once we were absolutely satisfied, the body was placed into a casket and our paperwork, including all of our findings, and a disc of photographs taken were placed in with them. These of course were the crucial missing pieces of evidence during my time at Fulham, which meant that further examinations had been necessary. To comply with International transportation of bodies the victims were treated with preservative granules, like sand, just ladled over the surface of the body. This prevented further body putrefaction and was much less dangerous than the embalming fluids, which had caused us so many problems at Fulham. During the first repatriation I was involved with in Thailand, I watched with amazement as the local undertaker sealed the body in a zinc-lined casket, closing the lid with an old fashioned soldering iron. It took him about eight minutes to do this. It ensured that the casket was leak-proof, essential for international transportation. Watching this, I was struck by a flash of inspiration. There was an issue around maintaining the sterility and condition of the paperwork that I was sending back with the body. To put it directly inside the casket with the body would not have been a good idea, but from this I realised that we could place these 'dry' items in an envelope and tape it to the outside of the zinc lid and on the underside of the wooden casket lid. It worked a treat.

So, the idea was that upon receipt of the victim at Fulham, the Coroner would be afforded the opportunity to read the paperwork and view the photographs, before deciding on the extent, if any, of any further examinations to establish Identification that she may require. The system actually did provide the weight of evidence in the majority of subsequent repatriations, for the Coroner to accept the evidence presented and negate the need for further examinations. This process remained in place until the closure of the Thailand Tsunami mortuaries in 2006.

***

One of my many learning points in Thailand was that I didn't factor in enough 'down time'. We worked long hours and this, combined with the nature of the work, meant that very special relationships were forged. I met some wonderful and extremely talented people whilst there and every now and again we managed to debrief over a beer at a local pub called The Whispering Cock, or as it was affectionately known to the DVI teams, 'John's Bar'. John was an ex-pat who had married a Thai girl and they had been settled in Thailand for a number of years. His bar was a great watering hole and served an essential purpose as a decompression chamber for stressed DVI workers.

One night we did steel ourselves away for a 'proper night out' venturing to the 'happening place', Patong. As we walked along the infamous Bangla Road we were accosted by dozens of Thai girls (at least I think most of them were girls), who asked: "You DVI? Which DVI you from?" I was impressed with their grasp of our terminologies. They never offered sex, it was more tasteful than that, and not at all as seedy as some may imagine. It was truly fascinating to me to see how it was done in a society that accepts prostitution – although technically speaking, prostitution is against the law in Thailand- and I spent a wonderful evening people watching and chatting with the locals but nothing more.

I had mixed feelings when it came to the end of my deployment. A new team of DVI trained officers from South Yorkshire were due to fly in and take over from the South Wales team. They arrived on the Friday, got settled and shadowed the South Wales team on the Saturday, learning the process and making sure that everything was handed over as smoothly as possible. Sunday was our day off before flying back to the UK on the Monday. The Saturday night turned out to be a great goodbye as the Rugby Union game between England and Wales was televised and although England lost, it was a great night in which I became a minor hero, managing to secure a special dispensation so that we could consume alcohol on what was supposed to be an alcohol-free national holiday.

On Sunday, a little worse for wear, the team chartered a boat and we went out to 'James Bond Island,' where some of the climatic scenes from *The Man with the Golden Gun* had been filmed. It was truly idyllic, and I started to realise just how hard we'd been working – almost three weeks of fourteen-hour-plus days – and I thought that never again in my life would I work so flat out. Sunday evening was spent preparing, both physically and mentally, to go home. Although I was sad to be leaving I was desperately looking forward to seeing Karon and the family. I was all geared up when there was a knock on my door.

It was one of the UK cops dealing with logistics for the operational deployment. The gist of what he said was: "You're not flying home tomorrow. All of the South Wales team are booked on the flight but we forgot about you Dick. The next flight is on Wednesday." I was absolutely devastated. I wanted to travel back as part of the team I had been working with. We were supposed to be all getting 'looked after' together; business class travel, quick access through customs, cars to pick us up and take us home. I don't think I've ever felt so alone. I didn't belong anywhere or with anyone. I felt like an 'also ran' and for the next few days I was going to be redundant. I couldn't go back to work because of the regulations. So I sat around the pool in the sun. This was not as idyllic as it sounds. It was absolutely dreadful, in fact. There was no one else around the pool, no tourists, nobody. The place was like a ghost town, particularly during the day when the DVI teams were at work. I hated every minute. I had gone from a million miles an hour to 5mph and had no one to talk with. It was really stressful.

By the time Wednesday came I was like a tightly wound clock. When I eventually did get on the long haul flight for home, I found that I was sitting next to a software engineer, totally unconnected with my line of work. Part of the diffusing process in DVI is to be able to talk with people, to be able to unwind and let it all out. Of course the nature of the work dictates that those people, whom one can speak with, are fairly restrictive. As a result DVI staff tend to diffuse with one another or at least with other Police employees or those within a similar line of work. I was just getting more and more wound up. When I landed back at Manchester there was no one there to meet me. I had to ring Karon to come and pick me up. This meant that I was left ticking away for another ninety minutes.

When I eventually arrived home my boss called and thanked me for my contribution before instructing me to take the next five days off. I almost screamed at him. I didn't want to. I desperately needed interaction and to share my experiences with colleagues but I wasn't allowed. There was nothing available in terms of welfare, no mechanisms in place for counselling as incredibly, even though we were in the year 2005, needing that kind of thing was still seen by some bosses as a sign of weakness. So I took it upon myself to meet up with an old friend who was a retired detective but who had assisted in Occupational Health. I had an 'off the record' chat with him for a couple of hours and he came up with a non-clinical diagnosis for what I was feeling as 'from pedestal to obscurity.' One minute I had been 'it', everyone was looking to me for advice and guidance and I was in a good position and in control. The next I was nothing. It was the psychological equivalent of jumping off a merry-go-round at 100mph. Because I was so closed down by my work environment, it took me over a year to admit the post-incident affect it all had on me. How stupid not to have been able to talk and share straight away? You can't operate at such high levels like that with no weaning and be ok. I realised the straw that broke the camel's back was that two days alone in paradise. It exposed me as not being super human – which cops like to think they are – and when we realise that we're not, our world comes crashing down around us. I really struggled. Crucially though, learning like this was invaluable, and one of my primary objectives on all subsequent training of DVI personnel was to highlight my experience, expose my own limitations and to provide advice on coping strategies post deployment.

I really struggled and for a long time I didn't really talk about what I'd been through. I learned that reflection carried out on one's own is a real danger indeed, it's incredibly hard to write about it now, for example. I just bottled up until I saw a TV documentary broadcast on the first anniversary of the disaster. The interviewer spoke to a man and his children who had lost their mother in Thailand. I knew her. I had been involved with her identification process at Fulham.

I had repeated my very first mistake at Dunkeswick and I completely fell apart.

***

In Thailand alone, over 8,000 victims were processed. 60% of the identifications were confirmed using odontology, 19% using fingerprints, 19% using dentistry and fingerprints together and 2% using DNA. DNA was valuable but was difficult to harness and audit.

Out of the 151 British Nationals who died in Thailand, all but six were recovered and identified. Lord Falconer , the then Lord Chancellor, announced, after petitions made by the families of the missing, that the usual seven-year rule would be waived in the case of the Asian Tsunami.

According to the Missing Persons Bureau, the seven-year rule states that: "for up to seven years after a person has last been seen, the court presumes that the person is still alive. After seven years, a court may allow a missing person's affairs to be dealt with, provided that: there are persons who would be likely to have heard of the missing person during that period; those persons have not heard of the missing person; and reasonable attempts have been made to find the missing person. If, however, there have been indications that the person was alive within those seven years, the passing of time, in itself, will not be enough for the court to assume that the missing person is dead."

Under the amended rule for the Asian Tsunami, the Coroner had to be satisfied that:

There was good evidence that the missing person was in the disaster area when the tsunami struck.

There was good evidence that the missing person was of sound mind i.e., he/she wasn't planning to 'disappear' to start a new life, as so many people do.

There had been no evidence of any activity relating to their daily life since the date of the disaster i.e., use of credit card, passport, etc.

In such cases, the families of the missing, and presumed dead, only had to wait one year before applying for a death certificate. Without a death certificate, claiming life insurance, re-organising mortgages and selling property registered in the name of the missing person is impossible. The State of New York adopted a similar approach, reducing their three-year-rule to one year for the families of the victims of the September 11 attacks.

Many of the bodies recovered after the Asian Tsunami, maybe up to a third, were those of children: babies, toddlers and teenagers. Numerous pregnant women were also victims. This disaster had been unimaginably cruel but, to do the job I had to keep my emotions in check and focus on the logistics of what needed to be done. Since coming home I have a massive trigger for real upset, even today. If a person tells me they knew someone who died in the Tsunami for example, when they start to show photographs of their loved ones it wrenches at my heart and pulls me straight back into that personal sphere – too personal and that's when I want to be able to hit an off-switch and stop all the memories, the images and the dark thoughts that come crashing in.

SEVENTEEN
BODY FARM

I never thought that DVI would take me to the United States but in May 2005, as a member of the Government's Mass Fatality Working Group, I was asked to go to Knoxville, Tennessee to observe an exercise run by the Disaster Mortuary Operational Response Team (DMORT).

It was of particular interest because this exercise involved a specialist wing of DMORT, which was simply subtitled as Weapons of Mass Destruction (DMORT/WMD), which specialised in the decontamination and examination of victims for mass fatality incidents caused by WMD's. With the rise of a new kind of terrorism since 9/11, the UK government was keen to prepare for the worst-case scenario.

My remit was to observe the exercise and write a comprehensive report. The exercise was going to take place on the outskirts of Knoxville, using cadavers from the world famous Body Farm, situated at the rear of Tennessee's main hospital, the University of Tennessee Medical Center.

We don't have anything like a Body Farm in the UK, partly because people have been opposed to the idea on grounds of taste and partly due to arguments about where such a facility might be sited. We do have something, however, to help scientists better understand the science of taphonomy (the study of decaying organisms): a pig body farm. More than one in fact, truly surreal places where you can see dead pigs wrapped in duvets, in cars, under trees, half-buried in damp soil, etc., etc.

In the US, thanks to novels and TV shows, the Body Farm has become "popular." Staff used to have to rely on a limited supply of dead bodies of unidentified vagrants but today they're overwhelmed with people wanting to donate their bodies, so much so that there's a waiting list – I'm not sure how this works exactly but I presume deep-freezing is involved. Several British scientists believe that the UK will one day get its own body farm. They argue that the body farm in Tennessee works well but can't help the UK because their flora and fauna of Tennessee is so different.

Needless to say, I was highly excited at the chance to visit DMORT, the Federal responders to DVI in the USA, as its international reputation was second-to-none in terms of cutting-edge science and having had the experience of dealing with the aftermath of some extraordinary and world famous terrorist attacks, such as the Oklahoma Bombing in 1995, which killed 168 and injured over 680, as well as 9/11.

I flew from Manchester to Chicago O'Hare airport on a scheduled 9-hour flight, arriving at 2pm in the midst of one of the worst rainstorms Chicago (a city known for its rain) has ever seen. I wondered how my aircraft had managed to land safely. My connecting flight, a small plane that would take me to Knoxville, was due to leave at 4.30pm with a flight time of three hours. The exercise briefing was scheduled for 10am the following morning, and this would be followed by a visit to the Body Farm and the actual exercise would start 9am the day after that. It was expected to finish at 3pm and would be followed by a 'hot debrief' – 'hot' means that it takes place onsite immediately afterwards. I was then scheduled to fly home on the evening of the fourth day of my trip, which just left me enough time to question the various members of the DMORT team.

It now looked as if the rain was going to throw my carefully orchestrated plans out of the window. All outgoing flights had been suspended, so I sat in a café and watched a spectacular thunderstorm erupt over Chicago. I had never seen anything like it. It was epic, biblical; so much lightning it was blinding, so much rain you couldn't see more than fifty metres. I started to doubt that I would ever make it to Knoxville. Finally, at 3am, after a thirteen-hour delay, the authorities decided that it was safe to resume flights. The larger trans-Atlantic flights had already started flying but I was travelling on a small plane with a maximum capacity of sixty passengers, so they'd sensibly decided to clear the backlog of larger planes first, while the conditions gradually improved.

I had been awake for 26 hours and was desperately tired but somewhat rejuvenated by the possibility of making it to Knoxville in time, I gratefully boarded the aircraft which was all set to take off at 3.30am. Seated in Row 1, I thought that at least I'd be first off the plane, and would hopefully arrive at my hotel at 7.30am, so I'd still be in time for this once-in-a career opportunity. The flight was three hours, and I'd managed with less than three hours' sleep plenty of times before in my police career, so settled down as the captain made profound apologies for the 'unavoidable' delay. He went on to explain that the severe weather front was now moving away from Chicago, to the south, and this had allowed air traffic to resume. My eyes snapped open. Did he say south? Geography was my favourite subject at school and I knew we would be flying south. I also presumed that we'd be flying faster than this weather front and would therefore quickly catch up with it. I tried to relax, told myself that the pilot would fly around it, or that the storm was headed southeast, and we were heading southwest, and started to doze.

I awoke with a bang, as if someone had picked me up and thrown me back down on my seat. We had entered the storm and it was like being on a very bumpy road, mixed with an extreme version of that weightless-stomach sensation you get when driving over a small hump-backed bridge. Announcements were made about seatbelts and no in-flight service, we were strapped in for the duration. My need for sleep was quickly forgotten, especially when the captain announced we were nearing the "eye of the storm" but "not to worry" as he had received clearance to try and fly over the worst section.

I sat there, helpless and more worried than I'd ever been in my life. Like most people, I try not to think planes crashing when flying. I told myself that the stats show that flying is the safest way to travel but this thought was quickly replaced by abject terror when a lightning bolt hit the plane, turning everything a blinding electric blue, accompanied by an explosion, as though the plane had been blown to pieces. I'm not particularly religious, although we went to church each Sunday when I was a boy, but I immediately renewed my faith and blurted out a very fast and very short prayer under my breath. I thought that this was 'it' and that my death would be an ironic one (and probably how I would be remembered), as my remains would be pieced together and identified by American DVI experts from DMORT.

Things didn't improve much even after I realised the plane was still intact. We now seemed to be on something that was a cross between a white water raft and a rollercoaster; my natural human instincts of fight or flight had kicked in but, being strapped in, I was only able to sit helplessly in terror, like everyone else, watching the plane bend and shake; despite our horror ride the passengers, myself included, were strangely silent, except for those moments where the plane plunged like a broken lift and a few people instinctively cried out in shock. The galley, which was just in front of me only added to the effect as it rattled and shook like an out-of-control washing machine loaded with tin cans. I then caught the eye of the flight attendant who was facing me, and we recognised the terror frozen on each other's faces. All we could do was hope for survival. This was out of our control. God only knows what the pilots – the only ones who could save the lives of sixty people – were feeling at that moment. I was helpless and powerless and I felt the tenacity drain from my body. A normally confident, determined, and motivated individual, my fatigue had sapped my strength and I started to feel extremely negative about the outcome. My mind became more irrational as I thought about the exercise I would never get to see, and that would probably be cancelled thanks to the disaster that was surely now imminent. For the first and only time of my life I told myself that I was ready to die and, I can only speak for myself, but perhaps in these moments, we are somehow able to prepare and come to terms with death. I felt ready. Sure enough, we were at that moment hit by another thunderbolt and this time the plane dropped like a stone; I recalled we were over land and that the flight path took us over Memphis and I wondered if we were anywhere near Graceland, the home of Elvis. Maybe we'd crash into it. Then I thought of my family; what would they do without me? And this was immediately followed by thoughts of Karon, my new wife, my exciting job, all the things I was passionate about and my will to live was suddenly rekindled. I said another prayer: "Please spare me as I've still got so much to give. Please let me finish my work." Of course, my work would never be finished, but this plea from the heart was based on my passion for life, family and for my work.

The captain then got on the PA system to say we'd been struck by lightning, which I'm sure led to a mental chorus among the passengers of something like: "No shit, Sherlock!" His voice had lost all the usual reassurance all pilots seem to have. It was shaking, cracking and he was speaking rapidly, under strain, as though he was still struggling to control the plane. He then said the lightning had done no damage to the plane – as far as he could tell- but, as casually as possible, he added: "I have decided that it is no longer safe for us to proceed on our current course and have received permission to land at the nearest airport, which is Nashville."

My barometer of terror was the face of the flight attendant and when I saw the relief I thought we must have a good chance. Unfortunately, my mental bunting was quickly packed away when we began our descent and started ping-ponging our way through black clouds thick with water and electricity. I started to sweat as my brain, which seemed to be suddenly determined to throw un-reassuring data into my consciousness, discharged the fact that most plane disasters occur during take-off and landing. How slippery was the runway? Could it be flooded? Would the undercarriage come down? Suppose the instruments were off, malfunctioning because of the lightning strike? I looked out of the window but it was pitch black, no sign of land. It took another twenty-five minutes before the pilot informed us landing was imminent and when those wheels thudded into the tarmac and the plane started to slow, the cabin erupted in applause, not just in thanks to the captain and the co-pilot but sheer, utter relief and joy that we were alive. We were alive! I clapped as if Rotherham had just won the Cup and thanked my maker, determined that I would fill my promise.

It had been at that moment, when I was certain I was going to die that I realised what I wanted most from my life: To share it with my family, to be with and cherish every day with Karon and, of course, do the absolute best for the world of DVI.

A few minutes later, as we were still taxying our way to the disembarking gate that I remembered where I was (the USA) and what I was supposed to be there for (a major DMORT exercise) and a series of questions burst into my mind in quick succession:

How would I get to Knoxville?

When would I get there?

When would I sleep?

How much of the exercise would I miss?

I started to panic. Perhaps it was a mixture of fatigue, adrenaline and God knows what else but it is amazing how quickly we forget to be thankful simply to be alive and able to appreciate the world and people around us. We are all alive and sharing this world together and it seems to me as though we spend far too much time worrying about things that don't matter. I think that disasters like the Tsunami remind us of this and this is why, when disasters happen, you see the absolute best of what humanity has to offer. I truly believe that people are wonderful but we get so caught up in the minutiae of everyday life that we lose sight of the big picture, as I did just a few minutes after I thought I was plummeting to a certain death.

It was 5am when we disembarked into a near-deserted airport. Two hours after that, with no refreshments available, a coach arrived to take us to Knoxville, which was three hours away. I was gutted. I was going to miss day one of the exercise but more disappointingly, I was going to miss my chance to visit the body farm.

It was 10am when I finally got into Knoxville. I called Steve Tinder, the head of DMORT to explain my plight. "Don't worry, Dick," he said cheerfully. "I'll brief you over dinner tonight."

It was with great relief that I crept into bed at 11am, after 32 hours without sleep. I awoke six hours later feeling refreshed and ready to go. I met Steve and we went with the other invited observers for dinner in Knoxville. Everyone was interested to hear about my brush with death and to be perfectly honest, I needed the debrief, so held court as I narrated my story to the other guests, who'd come from other parts of the US and Europe, none of whom I'd met before. Goodness knows what they made of this excitable Englishman with the funny accent.

The next day went as planned and the DMORT exercise was fascinating at least for me. Unfortunately, a confidentiality agreement, along with security reasons – we don't want to give terrorists any tips – prevents me from divulging details of the exercise. I wrote a twenty-page report upon my return, to assist in the UK planning for dealing with contaminated victims following mass fatality incidents. Although I've been involved in the joint planning for the examination of victims of such incidents, I would not have been deployed at the forefront of such an operation. That, along with victim recovery, would be undertaken by specialist CBRN-trained staff (Chemical, Biological, Radiological and Nuclear) from the government's CBRN team based at Winterbourne Gunner in Wiltshire.

After everyone had been debriefed, I mentioned to Steve how gutted I was to have missed out on the trip to the Body Farm. To my delight he immediately offered to take me around first thing in the morning, before my flight later that day.

The entrance, behind Knoxville's main hospital, was quite unobtrusive; an eight-feet tall solid door which, when closed, forms part of the perimeter fence. There was no grand sign, just a small painted board that said 'Research Facility. Biohazard. No trespassing.' I have to confess I felt a little disappointed as I was expecting something grander. Once inside, it reminded me of a huge allotment next to a small wood. A well-worn dirt path took the visitor through the site, and I saw body parts kept out in the open and in different everyday environments, e.g., inside a shed kept at twenty degrees centigrade; inside a car boot; covered in concrete or left in the open air.

The facility records details of what happens to the bodies/ body parts as part of its research. Photography, sometimes time lapse was used to help observe the rate of putrefaction and also to monitor the different types of wildlife that showed interest in a particular body, and at what stage.

I quickly forgot about the 'no frills' look of the Body Farm and became absorbed by their fascinating work at this incredibly sophisticated scientific anthropological research establishment. I knew that the bodies were either unidentified John and Jane Does, or were bequeathed to the facility by Body Farm fans, but what I didn't know was what the Body Farm did when it was finished with them. I asked and Steve pointed out a small cemetery.

"They're given a proper burial right here, on site, once they've fulfilled their purpose."

Many of the graves were unknown, bodies without an identity, with no past, no story. I was struck by the thought how some of these unknowns must have felt isolated and perhaps useless in their lives but in their deaths, they had done so much for modern forensic science.

All I need to say about my return journey is that it passed without incident.

EIGHTEEN
THE GREATEST REGRET

Throughout my life, as far as my job goes at least, I've always managed to be in the right place at the right time. The one time I was in the wrong place at precisely the wrong time was one of the worst periods I've ever had to live through.

It was a beautiful morning in early July and I was in the departure lounge of Manchester airport. I'd been asked to be the face of the UK police's disaster response and mass fatality management team by the organisers of an international conference to be held in Canada. It was a once-in-a-lifetime opportunity to address an audience of over 2,000 delegates and inform them how the UK dealt with DVI. I would meet with others like me – my international counterparts – and perhaps work with them towards establishing an international methodological consistency. Receiving an invitation was also a great honour; after all, it was the recognition of my peers, so I must have been doing something right.

Since returning from Thailand, I'd settled back into my professional life. The DVI teams dealing with the Tsunami were expected to take another twelve to eighteen months before the identifications would be completed and although I would have gone back if asked, I was relieved not to have to go as I was still finding it hard to "come down". I'd had an amazing experience; in terms of DVI management it couldn't have gone any better. I'd helped to establish procedures and systems and everything was working well. Advisors from MDAT travelled out to the disaster site regularly to check everything was running well, and I spent my days briefing the DVI teams who were about to be deployed, so they arrived as ready as could be. When I wasn't briefing I was working on London's Mass Fatality Plan, created to provide an integrated emergency response to instances involving mass casualties in London, including a massive evacuation plan. This plan, developed by the London Regional Resilience Forum (LRRF, now the London Resilience Team), a partnership of London's key responders, was supposed to ensure that London was well prepared to deal with any emergency, including a coordinated and multi-site attack. The role of the LRRF was tested as part of Atlantic Blue, an international exercise that took place in April 2005. The scenario in this exercise included multiple attacks on the underground system and was used to get people used to their roles.

When the Canadians got in touch, and asked for me to speak at the world disaster management conference, I wanted to shake their hand off with enthusiasm, but my eagerness was met coolly by the powers that be in the UK, who took some persuading that this was hugely important in terms of international recognition of the UK's efforts in DVI, and in the future development of this field. Finally, having been given the green light, I was booked to speak on July 9, 2005 in Toronto.

I was going over my keynote address in the airport lounge when I noticed 'Breaking News' flashing up on the silent TV screens that played *BBC News 24* day and night: Explosion on London Underground.

I stopped what I was doing and watched. Eventually, just as I was called to board the flight, my phone rang. It was a senior officer from the Met, asking for my help.

I rang my boss. "I'm at Manchester airport about to get on the plane but I could be in London in under four hours."

"No," he replied. "You've been promised to the conference. You have to go. You can give advice on phone once you're there."

And I stepped onto the plane.

As soon as I disembarked I knew I'd made the wrong decision. The screens playing 24-hour news channels in Toronto airport told me that the explosions had been part of coordinated terrorist attacks. My phone started to ring the moment I switched it on. The only place I wanted to be was in London but instead I was thousands of miles from home, receiving phone calls from people on the front line of this disaster who needed my advice. I couldn't believe it. The London Mass Fatality plan had only just been signed off two weeks earlier.

I was pleased to learn that the duty of overseeing mortuary management had been passed to the capable hands of Sergeant Kevin Gordon from the British Transport Police – Kevin, you will remember, was Chief Mumper at Fulham Mortuary during the first few weeks after the Tsunami, and would be officially commended for his efforts after the 7/7 bombings – but I still felt like a spare wheel on the wrong side of the planet as I briefed the international press for about an hour. All they wanted to know about was what was happening in London. All I could say was: "Please don't ask about London, I can say what will be happening, but nothing specific to the incident."

CBS News didn't hold back: "Mr. Venables you're billed here as one of the top DVI men from Great Britain and London is experiencing terrorism and mass fatalities as we speak now. Can you tell me why you are here at a conference rather than in England now where you are needed?"

This quadrupled the guilt I was already feeling. I did my best to reply, stating that I was on my way here when it happened and as such was directed to conduct business here.

"I will get involved ASAP upon my return," I told them. I continued to receive lots of calls, mainly from workers asking me for advice on practical things, such as the filling out of the Interpol forms.

I wish I hadn't listened, I wish I'd never gone to Canada. I locked myself in my hotel room and continued to take dozens of calls, mainly from on-scene workers. My phone simply did not stop. I didn't realize how much of an expert I'd become since that first day almost a decade earlier in Dunkeswick. I gave up on Canada, flew back and went straight to the emergency mortuary.

If the demands of a mass fatality incident exceeded the capabilities of the local or regional arrangements (as was the case with 7/7) then the Coroner would ask for the deployment of NEMA (National Emergency Mortuary Arrangements). NEMAs are set up at sites previously chosen by local authorities. Central London's emergency site were in the grounds of the Honourable Artillery Company (part of the British Army Reserve) in the City of London.

The so-called 'mortuary village' had been set up in under 24 hours, a remarkable achievement, and this was testament to the NEMA arrangement. It included a post-mortem suite with six fully-equipped workstations, as well as areas for ontological assessment, fluoroscopy, radiology, photography, and Scenes of Crime Officers (SoCOs) to work. Importantly, each bombsite was designated a separate area to avoid cross-contamination. There were separate reception and storage areas for the deceased, office accommodation, meeting rooms, canteen, staff changing rooms and a personal protection equipment collection point. Up to 250 staff could be on site at the same time.

It was perfect.

Disaster Action were on hand to act as lay advisers to the friends and families of the victims. They became involved in their invited capacity at the Family Assistance Centre (now called Humanitarian Assistance Centres), which opened within 48 hours of the attacks. Their role was crucial as people waited for news of loved ones (a viewing area had been established in readiness for friends and family as identifications were made).

A total of 52 people died at the four bombsites, plus the four suicide bombers. About 700 people were injured with 22 in serious or critical conditions. Recovery of the dead was not going to be straightforward. The two sides of the evidential recovery had to be balanced: the DVI teams would focus on victim recovery and identification while officers from SO13 (counter terrorism, now SO15) would concentrate on the criminal investigation. Fortunately, SO13 officers now had a good understanding of DVI and knew that a coordinated deployment of DVI staff alongside specially-trained counter terrorist crime scene investigators would work well in terms of identifying the perpetrators (and possibly their support networks), as well as properly identifying and repatriating the innocent victims killed in the attack.

Four teams were deployed to the sites to recover the deceased and to simultaneously forensically recover the bomb scenes. Each recovery team consisted of the following:

Two DVI officers.
One SO13 exhibits officer and team leader, who would exhibit all items recovered, including the deceased.
Two SO13 officers.
One photographer.

The delay in body recovery attracted a great deal of criticism from the media and public but the recovery teams found themselves operating in dangerous conditions. Working underground, hundreds of metres along overheated tunnels, which were full of dust and debris, possibly on the verge of collapse, and in the knowledge that there may be unexploded secondary devices yet to be discovered, was unimaginably difficult.

Also, SO13 had to perform detailed forensic examinations to retrieve any material used to produce the bombs, or any material that may help to identify the perpetrators. This included tiny fragments that could easily have been lost or be accidentally removed from the scene and without which those responsible may not have been traced.

Another major problem that led to delays was mortuary transport. The mortuary vans attended all sites on rotation and took several hours to negotiate the even busier than normal London traffic – the public transport network having pretty much been shut down. This was unfortunate and would be corrected in future, especially as this could have led to cross-contamination between the four crime scenes.

The first body arrived at the temporary holding area on the evening of July 8. Dr. Robert Chapman from Fulham was the lead pathologist and coordinated the post mortem procedures, which ran from 8am to 8pm every day.

Digital and computed radiography was used for the first time to assist with victim identification. The field of forensic radiography is another relatively new forensic discipline with enormous promise for mass fatality incidents. Radiography is the use of a specific range of electronic radiation to view objects, animals or humans. Radiology is a medical specialty that uses an image to diagnose trauma and pathological conditions and can be applied in some instances to treat patients. Radiologists are medically-qualified personnel who report the radiological findings from the images produced by a radiographer. These images might also be examined by other forensic specialists, i.e., a forensic pathologist, forensic odontologist or a forensic anthropologist.

Radiological investigations are used to confirm the identity of the living and deceased subjects, to identify suspected non-accidental injury and to help determine and confirm the cause of death and the location of foreign bodies. It aids in the detection of injuries, identification of pathological conditions, as well as the discovery of foreign objects that may be hazardous to the practitioners, that may be of evidential value, or may be useful for identification purposes (surgical implants, dental artefacts, and personal effects). It can also be used to analyse the contents of a body bag before opening.

The equipment used for mass fatality incidents is lightweight and easily assembled and includes two mobile image intensifiers (C–Arms) for fluoroscopic examinations; two mobile imaging tables; one direct digital mobile x-ray unit; one mobile imaging table and two mobile direct digital dental imaging systems.

Fluoroscopy is an imaging technique used to obtain real-time images of objects using a fluoroscope, which allows well-defined x-rays to be played and recorded on a monitor from which print outs can be made. Fluoroscopy can be used to check for explosives and other hazardous material; rapid charting of fragmentary remains; the location of personal effects; location and documentation of projectiles and fragments in situ as well as the location and documentation of other items of evidence.

Digital x-ray imaging systems are the same as the traditional ones we're used to seeing in hospitals, except they record digital images and are therefore faster and easier to view. In a mass fatality situation digital radiography is used for examination of the skeleton, establishing projectile pathways, evaluating age at death, investigating and recording ante-mortem trauma and establishing and identifying features.

Computed tomography (CT) uses x-rays in conjunction with computing algorithms to create 3D image of the body. These images are particularly useful for the evaluation of trauma. CT is fast and yields valuable information relating to identification, health and safety, autopsy planning and cause of death. The use of CT scanners has been labelled by some as 'vir-topsy' as bodies can be examined internally without cutting. Current research is directed towards a mass fatality mortuary of the future, which will be run by radiographers with images being beamed directly to experts who can analyse them from their desks.

In the wake of 7/7, a team of radiologists working within the PM suite compared PM images with those taken from potential victims' ante-mortem medical records. This helped identify foreign objects, which had to be extracted and examined in case they were part of one of the bombs.

Cause of death in all cases was decreed to be the same: a result of explosion. This meant that the vast majority of the bodies only needed an external examination. Dr. Chapman didn't keep exact figures but confirmed that the majority of victims were identified through odontology, followed by fingerprints, while a couple of identifications were made using DNA comparisons.

No viewings by family and friends of the victims took place until after the Identification Commission had concluded that victims' identities had been correctly established. The viewing required careful management between the mortuary managers and family liaison officers and the system as well as the viewing facilities receive praise from religious and community leaders as well as – most importantly – the victims' families. On average, families spent two hours in the viewing area.

Mistakes did take place, however. Staff vetting came into the fore when, on July 13, a British Transport Police officer was found checking body labels and behaving strangely; when questioned it emerged he had lost a family member in the bomb on the Piccadilly line. Staff always need to be checked for involvement, an issue I would encounter on my very next job.

That things had gone so well was thanks to our preparations, in particular the Mass Fatality Plan. Also, the Asian Tsunami had meant that London was even more ready than it could have been for an attack like this. The operation dealing with the identification and repatriation of UK citizens had been going for seven months by this time. Identification staff and systems were operating like well-oiled machines. It also helped that members of the senior command structure were familiar with each other and the processes required for effective Disaster Victim Identification.

I was pleased to see that all the elements I'd brought to the Mass Fatality plan had helped produce an effective response after the London bombings but I was still gutted not to have been the flag bearer for DVI on this most crucial occasion. It was then I realized that I'd begun my work in DVI and disaster management by making myself indispensable but, thanks to all the training I'd provided in the last few years, I wasn't indispensable anymore. I realized that I could not and should not always be in control and that I could stand back and let others get on with the job.

It was a terrifying time to be in London, especially when further attacks were attempted on 21 July. People didn't want to take the underground – myself among them – and there were long queues for taxis. I ended up walking between meetings most of the time and was strangely relieved when it was clear I was no longer needed – 'strangely' because I didn't like the feeling of not being needed, but I was relieved to be able to return home at last to South Yorkshire, where I could be with my family and find a way back into normal life, at least for a while.

NINETEEN

A DEATH IN MY LIFE

I retired from the police on March 6, 2006[6]. There was no party no gifts – apart from a standard decanter from the Police Federation and a certificate of good conduct – no celebrations, nor commiserations. I had no home in the police; my remit meant I simply roamed wherever the work took me. It was a strange departure after thirty years of service. The Monday after I left I continued to work as a private DVI consultant. There still wasn't enough training in DVI and disaster management in the police and like anyone I wanted to make sure my work had meaning and a life beyond mine. I wanted to make sure no one forgot their training, or stopped giving it, the worst thing for me would be for us to slip back to pre-2001 levels of DVI. We're fortunate in the UK to not have had a big incident since 7/7 but a big shout will come one day and we need to be match fit. It certainly wasn't a plan to get rich (and I never did), it was more about making sure I could carry on passing on the knowledge, and I wanted to stay in the loop and keep abreast of any developments in DVI. The subject had become an infectious passion for me and I was keen

---

6   I actually finished at end of October 2005 but I was owed so much leave that I was paid up to March 6, 2006.

to be involved in the training of others. The National Centre of Police Excellence continued to ask me to deliver SIM courses as a private contractor. So in the end, even though I'd left the police, nothing really changed on a day-to-day basis. Karon and I lived modestly – my police pension – of which Jen got half as part of the divorce settlement – was not enough to live from – but life was good, full of family and meaningful work that I loved. I eventually trained 4,000 cops, pathologists and Coroners and the Senior Identification Managers (SIMs) now take charge of Mass Fatality Coordination Groups, which are set up in the immediate aftermath of disaster.

***

A May Saturday in 2006. Karon and I were having the rarest of lie-ins when there was a knock at the door. I squinted at the bedside clock. 6.45am. We both pretended to be asleep but the knocker was persistent. Furious, I gave in, threw back the covers, stomped downstairs and yanked open the door.

"YES?" I demanded, momentarily taken aback by the fact that a man in well-cut, dark suit was on my doorstep at the crack of dawn on a Saturday.

"Are you Mr. Richard Ven-"

"Hang on a minute, who the hell do you think you are?"

"Sir, apologies, but I need to see some ID and then I require your signature."

"I'm in my own bloody house, and you're asking me for ID?" My eyes were like saucers.

He was holding a letter, which shook slightly in his hand. I assumed it was a speeding fine and so I stomped off to get a utility bill to prove who I was. I stared daggers and signed furiously, practically tearing through the paper.

"What the hell do you think you're doing, waking people at 7am on a Saturday morning?"

He looked really frightened. Good, I thought, slamming the door. I went back to bed, throwing the letter on the floor.

"Who was it?" Karon asked sleepily.

"I think I've been done for speeding!" I exclaimed, trying to get comfortable.

Karon got up and had a look at the envelope. She opened it.

"Rich," she said, "I think you're going to want to see this."

"Christ, what is it then? What have I been done for and what's it going to cost me?"

"Take a look!"

So I did. I saw the official headed paper of HRH the Queen and frowned in confusion. I looked at Karon. She grinned at me. I started to read.

"Bloody hell!"

I was in the Queen's 80th birthday honours list. A Queen's Police Medal!

I felt terrible for that poor man; that probably wasn't the kind of reaction he was used to. I quickly looked out of the window to see if he was still there so I could apologise but he was long gone. Obviously he felt no need to hang around the house of a total psycho any longer than he had to. It was a good job I was lying down, I was in total shock at the news, euphoric. The hardest part was keeping it secret for three weeks until the official announcements were made.

The Queen's Police Medal for Distinguished Service was given to me for my work in establishing DVI as a nationally recognised field of operations and being involved in various DVI operations under special difficulties.

I went with Karon and Mum and Dad to the Palace on 24 November 2006. Only five of the hundred people honoured that day were getting the QPM and the others were cops who were doing so because they'd achieved high rank. It was – and still is – rare for a police officer of my rank to receive this honour. I was so nervous, even though we rehearsed.

"Say Ma'am as in jam and don't curtsey," I was advised and waited in the ante-room until my name was called: "Richard Venables, Lately Detective Inspector of the National Centre for Police Excellence." Suddenly I found myself walking towards the Queen, telling myself to bow not curtsey, and suddenly noticing that my mouth was impossibly dry. When my turn came HRH asked me to explain my job, which I duly did.

"Tell me," HRH said. "Why are you 'lately' of the police?"

"I've retired Ma'am."

"Retired?" the Queen asked. "You don't look old enough. What are you going to do with yourself?"

I was taken aback. This was like being told off by my gran.

"Well, Your Majesty, I've accrued a lot of skills and experience which I feel duty bound to pass on to others."

"Yes, we need to do these things, don't we?"

I was briefed that when she offered her hand to shake I should reciprocate, as that was the signal that the conversation had come to an end.

At this point The Queen did exactly this, but as our hands locked together I felt her gently push me back, leaving me in no doubt that my time was up! Despite the shock of this ending, it was the best ordeal of my life and I backed away from Her Majesty with a huge grin on my face, buzzing with excitement. As I entered the next room a video camera caught my somewhat delightedly dazed expression before my medal, boxed and ready to go, was handed to me and I was free to go.

I received many congrats from senior officers but my favourites came from the rank and file officers like myself, with whom I'd worked over the years. They truly are the unsung heroes.

***

I continued training SIMs as I'd promised HRH, and a month later, I finished one course teaching twenty Detective Chief Inspectors and Superintendents finishing with the usual: "Major incidents are thankfully rare but at least one of you here will have to call upon these skills... Except for you Neil." Neil Hunter was a DCI from Lancashire Police and I'd declared him 'safe' seeing as Lancashire had had their disaster with the cockle pickers in 2004. I even went as far as excusing him from my summing up as I had assumed that lightning would not strike twice.

Two weeks later, on December 28 2006 my phone rang. It was Neil. "Remember you said it'll never be me. Well, you were wrong!"

A helicopter had crashed into Morecambe Bay, killing all seven crew. Six bodies had been recovered though one would never be found.

"Dick can you come out and run the mortuary with some trained staff?"

"I'm no longer in the police, Neil," I replied, "I work as a consultant now."

Neil said he'd pay whatever it took to get me there, so I charged half my normal day rate, because he needed me and I needed to be there. We spent one hour on the phone, which was the time it took him to travel to Blackpool Police Station from his home. During that time we went through the 'golden hour' issues for the SIM to consider. I know he was grateful and reassured by that conversation.

I arrived at the De Vere Hotel in Blackpool that night – the bodies had been taken to the Blackpool Victoria Hospital – and was given the red-carpet treatment by the Lancashire Police who were genuinely pleased to have me on hand to advise.

The idea was to carry out all the victim examinations on the following day at the hospital mortuary, starting at 6am and working through until they were completed.

The helicopter had appeared to lose control while attempting to pick up workers from the North Morecambe gas platforms, approximately 24 miles from Morecambe Bay's shoreline. It had hit the sea with its main rotor still spinning at 400mph, and so the aircraft broke up on impact, with wreckage scattered over a wide area. All of the victims were wearing life jackets, but had been so severely injured in the impact that none had been able to inflate them. The three rescue boats sent to the scene did an amazing job in rough seas to recover six of the seven bodies. Although one person was missing, we did not foresee any difficulties with identification of those who had been recovered as we had a flight manifest with seven names and the bodies were intact, and in survival suits.

As I arrived at the hospital mortuary, a police officer, somewhat belligerently I felt, came up to me and said: "You want a quick way to ID them? They're all in survival suits; each one has a unique number and barcode for each person. Job done."

I thanked him but there was no way I was going to rely on that and, sure enough, it turned out that the two tallest men were each wearing the other's suit. If we'd relied solely upon this, we would have ended up showing the wrong bodies to the families.

Later that same day, as we painstakingly worked our way through the victims, one of my staff suddenly declared that he knew one of the victims and questioned the need to detail all items on the body when he could clearly identify him. I was shocked that a member of my team had known a victim but hadn't declared the fact before we'd begun the DVI process. I removed him and discussed this revelation with Neil. Ultimately, it was up to Neil as SIM (and the officer) if he wanted to carry on. To my amazement, they decided that he should. My view was most definitely that he shouldn't have been in there. This was something else that I decided to build into DVI best practice. Now we always check every officer and DVI worker by asking: "Does anyone here know or is likely to know anyone likely to be in a body bag, or any of their relatives?"

By the time I returned to the hotel at 11.30pm I was exhausted, emotionally and physically. The victims had been identified using fingerprints and the Family Liaison officers had done excellent work finding latent prints through work colleagues. All of the deceased were married, many with children and I couldn't help but think that their Christmas's would be forever tainted by this terrible event. At least the families would be able to see their loved ones' bodies in the morning, I told myself, and that was the best result we could have hoped for.

As it was late, there was no one in reception. I rang the bell and waited. No one came. It was then that I noticed there were some people gathered to my right in an anteroom and I naturally wondered what they were up to, so late at night. Then I noticed they were all crying and, to my growing horror, I spotted one of the family liaison officers. It was the families. Good grief, we'd been put in the same hotel.

I couldn't tear myself away from looking at the widows of the men who had died and found myself trying to pair them with the deceased. I was appalled with myself. Why was I doing this? Why? It was so weird; I couldn't understand it. By the time the reception-ist turned up, I was on the verge of having a panic attack and I snatched my key and didn't dare wait for the lift. I ran up the stairs to my room where I broke down, the smell of death all around me.

* * *

At the debrief I was able to vent a little about being placed in the same hotel as the families and I received a heartfelt apology, which of course I naturally accepted. I was told it was a simple oversight – albeit with awful psychological consequences – and such a mistake would not be made again. Today there's a memorial to the dead of the Morecambe Bay Helicopter Crash sited on the promenade near Fleetwood Lifeboat Station in Morecambe. The victims were chief pilot, Captain Stephen Potton, 52, from Blackpool and co-pilot Simon Foddering, 33, from Preston; passengers Bob Warburton, 60, of Heysham, Lancs, Leslie Ahmed, 48, of South Shields, John Shaw, of Kirkcaldy, Fife, Scotland, and Alfred Neasham, 57, from Durham. The passenger still unaccounted for but presumed dead was Keith Smith, 57, from Stockton-on-Tees.

***

Dad was my hero. I had been so pleased that he had been able to come to the Palace to see me collect my QPM but unfortunately I couldn't really say how much he understood about the whole day because by this time, Alzheimers, the disease of our age, had him in its grip.

It had started with me being awoken by the phone at 3am. I suspected the worst – a disaster, I would be needed.

"Is that my commanding officer?"

"Excuse me?"

"Sergeant Venables here sir," the voice said, "The enemy's retreating. Is it safe for lights out?"

"Dad? Is that you? Do you know what time it is?"

"The enemy are retreating," he repeated. "Is it safe for lights out?"

"Er. Yeah. Yes. It is. Go to bed Dad."

"Yes sir. Lights out and we can sleep in the trenches."

"That's right the attack is over Dad, go back to bed."

Dad, who was 82, had had a heart attack when he was 77. This had brought it home to me that he wouldn't be around forever.

Then came the Alzheimers. As I said, Dad – Walter – was my hero. He and Mum (Mildred) were childhood sweethearts. They were courting in 1942 when Dad, just 20-years-old and working down the pits, was called up and sent to North Africa with the Royal Corps of Signals. Mum volunteered for the Women's Land Army, known as the Land Girls, and worked the land along with the 80,000 other women who replaced the agricultural workers who'd been called up to the military.

Like many men, Dad didn't like to talk about his war exploits but he had a personal letter signed by King George VI, framed and hanging over the fireplace commending his bravery and sometimes as a child, when I waxed enthusiastically about it, I could eventually wheedle stories out of him. Dad won six medals during World War II, including the Military Medal for bravery in the field after he established communications between two Allied divisions in Italy in 1944. Dad crossed rivers and pulled cables through countless streets while under constant shell and mortar fire – repeating the whole experience after it was irreparably destroyed, and then dashing back several times after that for repairs, always under attack – providing a vital link between two Allied divisions that saved many lives and changed the course of the battle for Italy.

Dad married Mum immediately upon his return in September 1945 and they moved in to Angel Street. Dad took up work as a storekeeper in the local colliery before becoming a stock control manager until his retirement in 1982. My eldest brother Robert was born in October 1947, followed by Michael three-and-a-half-years after that, and then I came along six years after Michael. Something that Dad and I shared (unlike my two older brothers) was a love of the beautiful game. He took me to my first Rotherham United match in 1962, when I was just four years old and I took to it like a duck to water. I have always been the sporty sibling, so enjoyed that special bond this love created with Dad. I continued this throughout my life, managing and coaching junior football and qualifying as a football referee during the nineties.

Robert, who was an out-and-out academic, became a barrister and is today one of the UK's most eminent Tax Silks. Like me, Michael joined South Yorkshire police and was also awarded the QPM in 2002 for distinguished service in relation to his work with ethnic communities. Like me, Michael isn't a gifted academic, and I think he felt pressured to try and reach the giddy heights of Robert's success.

As the youngest son, and having two eminently successful older brothers, I felt this pressure to succeed twice over. My parents didn't ever pressure me, they only supported me in whatever I wanted to do with my life but I always felt that, even if I achieved something, I was still lagging behind and always playing catch-up with my brothers.

All of us went to Wath Grammar School in South Yorkshire, which was under the supervision of headmaster Dr Clifford Saffell. On my second day in that school in September 1968, Dr Saffell called me to his office.

"Your brother, Robert is an exceptionally gifted student, one of the brightest boy that has passed through this school. And with that in mind, in the interest of fairness, I have instructed the staff never to compare your academic performance with his. If you ever experience any comparison, then report directly to me and I will see that it doesn't happen again."

My parents were friends with Dr Saffell and when I told them about his proclamation they agreed with him wholeheartedly. What I never revealed (until now) is that for the next seven years, teachers did nothing but compare my academic performance to that of Robert's, belittling my average academic achievements in the process. I didn't tell anyone because I felt doing so would mean I would get special treatment and I wanted to succeed on my own merits. That feeling of playing catch-up stayed with me for many years but, thank goodness, as my own career developed I came to realise that I have made a positive difference through my work as a police officer and most especially in DVI.

After his heart attack, the doctor advised Dad to stop the scotch, saying, "If you must drink, red wine is better." Dad's red wine started to get paler and paler each time I saw him – he was diluting it with more and more scotch. He stopped smoking – for a few hours – and then had crafty fags outside of the house.

Alzheimer's arrived when he was 82 and he forgot he drank, so that was the end of his red wine and scotch cocktail, but he continued to smoke, which was a worry as he once put the lit end of the cigarette in his mouth. Plus, there are all the other obvious flammable dangers associated with cigarettes. I'd seen the terrible results of too many clumsily-placed and half-extinguished cigarettes as a young police officer.

Mum became Dad's full-time carer and, once the Alzheimer's took hold, he started pushing her to the limit in terms of what she was able to endure. Eventually the family agreed that Dad needed to spend some time in a care home, for Mum's sake, if nothing else. I found this very hard to cope with. The home was lovely but you can't help but be upset by the experience.

Although I've seen more than anyone's fair share of dead bodies, before Hillsborough I'd only ever seen one person die right before my eyes, literally in front of me, and that was when I was eleven years old. My family used to go to St Michael's Church in Swinton. We were a small congregation, about 20–25 people. I was a 'server' and carried the incense among other spiritual items. Robert usually played the organ but on this occasion a new organist was having his debut and so all of his family came to the church to hear him play.

After taking Communion, the organist's grandma was walking back to the pew when she collapsed right in front of me and hit her head on the gas bottle that fed the church's heater. The crack echoed through the church. I watched the colour leave her face and her lips turn blue. There was no blood but I knew she was dead. Her expression was so different to someone just sleeping. Shock and upset spread among the parishioners, but I felt nothing. I continued to look at her. Like all children, I had been fed with stories of ghosts and evil spirits designed to cause of fear of dying and the dead but seeing this lady at peace, I thought: 'If that's what dying is then there is nothing to worry about; it's quicker and easier than falling asleep'.

But when it came to Dad's death, I was a mess. He broke his hip and then, after an operation, he started to deteriorate. Visits turned into vigils. Then, he started to fade at 9pm on Saturday April 11, 2009 with all the immediate family at his bedside. It was dramatic, almost like a film. I held his hand; it was cool but he was still breathing. He reached over to Mum and flinched, reacting to her. His breathing was even until he drew in a great breath, which was followed by some rasping and his body relaxed, then he repeated the cycle with the rasping decreasing each time. This continued until 2am. We were by this time exhausted to the point of unconsciousness, so we decided to take a cab the short distance home and return first thing in the morning. Dad officially died at 6.15am, shortly before we arrived. For me he passed away when he finally lost consciousness and stopped reacting to us. I will always deeply regret not being there at the moment of his death, and wish I'd managed to hang on for just a few more hours, but I was just too tired.

I dreaded Dad dying as, despite everything, I was totally inexperienced when it came to the physical act of dying. Since his death my fears have dissipated, I'm so much more at ease about it now, more relaxed, I've lost the fear but I don't quite understand why myself. Perhaps it is the realisation that death – the way my Dad died – is as natural as birth, but it's not a subject we like to drag out for discussion.

Although professionally I usually advocated for a full autopsy when Dad died, it changed things for me. The humanitarian side of death hit home. I didn't want them to do an autopsy on Dad and found myself lost in the wilderness as I hadn't dealt with this side of death, from the perspective of the grief-stricken relative. I took it like a novice. Dad had undergone an operation five weeks earlier so the Coroner ordered an autopsy to make sure medical negligence wasn't responsible. I was appalled. Having seen so many autopsies, I knew what would happen to Dad's body and although I wasn't present, I 'felt', every incision. This was a massive learning curve. I realised I had to be more cognizant of the bereaved; we should listen to families more.

I didn't view the body. No one in the family did. I didn't want to. I didn't need to. It helped that I'd known he was dying for a long time, so I was as well prepared as I could be and so I decided I wanted to remember Dad as he was in life.

In between Dad's death and the funeral, I was booked to give a Mortuary Managers' course in North Yorkshire. I don't know how I did it but somehow I managed to put myself into mega-professional mode. I worried about cracks or weaknesses showing during the course but somehow I made it through.

Mum had already invested in a family plot at the local cemetery in 2000; plot numbers 46, 47, 48. Mum and Dad were to go jointly in 47. The first time Dad had "seen" his resting place was when we buried him. Dad, a bona-fide War Hero, was given a full military funeral and there was a huge turnout. We were joined by his friends from the British Legion who arranged for the Last Post to be played at his graveside, which was incredibly emotional. I'd been struggling to contain myself when we bore his coffin to the grave and hearing the Last Post, well it was devastating. The Reverend Jack Harris, who conducted the ceremony was my brother Robert's friend from school, which made it a bit more personal and slightly easier to bear. There were so many people but I can't remember anything; the day passed in a blur of emotion.

I was weeping by the graveside when it suddenly dawned on me that I'd been working like mad trying to secure my finances for the future, always worrying about what was around the corner. Stuff that, I thought. Life is short. I needed to live a little before I moved in next to Dad.

My son Matthew was next to me. "You know what?" I told him. "I'm going to buy a black BMW convertible with a red interior next week."

"Why are you telling me this now?" Matt asked.

"Because if I don't, you'll be doing it when I'm in there," I said, pointing into the grave, "I'm going to spend your inheritance."

I bought that Black BMW two months later. My outlook on life has changed. Clichés are clichés for a reason, they do contain powerful truths and as the saying goes, I plan to live forever but live like I am going to die tomorrow. Having said that, living like you're going to die tomorrow sounds like a terribly stressful existence, so I have a more moderate version of that: I am careful about planning for the future but also remember to live for today. I love travel and so Karon and I now head off on holiday four times a year. When death comes, it's too late for regrets. I should know that better than most.

So, one of the things I did in terms of careful planning for the future was that I became the Chief Grave Plot Tenderer. I made a bit of a garden around the family plot (it's even got log roll edging), and tended my own grave. I go there once a week or so and talk to myself – and to Dad. It's maybe one of the most trite sayings about life but the world does continue to turn, life goes on after loss, and this thought comforted me – and was demonstrated to me thanks to the fact that Mum had put us under an apple blossom tree. This sounds lovely but I have to contend with tree roots and birds, which bring, well, you know. I have to clean Dad's headstone every week, which involves detergent and scrubbing. I have to do a good job, just like everything else in life. One day, I was scrubbing away when an old lady came to put flowers on the grave next to mine. It was her husband, who'd died in his 70s.

"You've got a big grave," she said with a smile.

Ok, I had to admit it looked a little over the top, with one headstone and all my edging and planting efforts. I explained.

"Oh, that's nice, I'm going into the plot next to my husband as well."

I looked down at our graves. "So we're going to be neighbours then."

I introduced myself and we shook hands. I then said to her jokingly, "If you bring the tea bags I'll bring the sugar, give me a knock and we can have a cup of tea."

The old lady looked at me strangely, said a quick and curt goodbye and started to walk off down the cemetery, occasionally glancing back over her shoulder at me, a puzzled look on her face. I never saw her again, above ground anyway. I arrived at our family grave one day in 2013 to see a new headstone in the adjoining plot. I couldn't help but think: "I wonder if she took the tea bags?"

EPILOGUE

RETURN

After the Tsunami, training really opened up. More and more Police Forces wanted DVI-trained officers and nationally there were moves to form a UK DVI cadre, which would be made up of officers who received enhanced training and who subsequently, were better equipped to be deployed overseas. I was hoping to become heavily involved in this training, despite my retirement from the Police. Bizarrely, I was retained to deliver the SIM training as a private consultant but not asked to deliver the training for the UK DVI team. My exclusion will always remain a mystery to me, although I have learned, over a period of thirty years that while the Police Service is great at producing experienced practitioners, they are poor when it comes to holding onto that talent and experience.

I continued to deliver the SIM training course until early 2009 when, just after Dad passed away, I received a letter from the head of Uniformed Operational Support at The National Police Improvement Agency (NPIA, now the College of Policing), essentially the new name for the National Centre for Police Excellence (NCPE). His department was responsible for delivering the SIM and Foundation DVI training to Police Forces in England and Wales but not the UK's national team, which fell to Dundee University, supported by CIFA and ACPO's lead on UK DVI.

I was told that I'd been "released" as of that moment. As my letter of termination said: "Since my arrival at the NPIA the Service has been keen to ensure that the delivery of training is done by occupational as well as operationally competent individuals. For the SIM this means having a person to deliver the training who is an accredited SIM and has experience within this field. Ownership of this course will be retained by the NPIA and as you are not an accredited SIM you services will no longer be required."

I had taught over three hundred senior officers to become SIMs but as I had retired, it had been argued, I could not be a SIM myself.

Instead, immediately after my departure, trainers without any real-world DVI experience were teaching my training programme. A lack of experience and confidence, I believe, has led to the abandonment of the ACPO Victim Profile Forms, which were only ever intended to provide a simpler, user-friendly alternative to the Interpol form in the case of domestic incidents. Unfortunately, we have now returned to the exclusive use of the overly-complex Interpol form which, despite my many submitted suggestions for improvement, retains practically the same format it has had for thirty years.

I was deeply upset at finding myself ostracized from the job I loved but such is the petty way of the police sometimes. I managed to continue to work as a consultant with those local police forces with whom I'd worked with in the past, but this work has gradually fallen away as my contacts retire or change roles. Two colleagues who continued to request me as their preferred trainer were Detective Superintendent Graham Yip from Merseyside Police and Inspector Iain Thomas from Gwent Police. Graham retired in 2012 and in the same year Iain relinquished DVI responsibilities for Gwent Police. I'd like to thank them both for their unstinting support; it was hugely appreciated.

I had lived and breathed DVI and disaster response for almost two decades, and did so because I believed I had found my calling and was totally passionate about it, no other reason. I was the most experienced person in the country in DVI mortuary work and still felt as though I had a great deal to give.

But, as I mentioned before, life goes on.

* * *

I had never really dealt with the mental trauma I'd been left with after having worked in Thailand under such extreme conditions. In a way, what I felt after Thailand was added to the sum of all the traumas I'd witnessed over my career and these threatened to break the damn of my unconscious. Don't get me wrong, I was never a gibbering wreck, I just got on with life, which I enjoyed, but there was always a dark cloud, just out of sight, full of unprocessed memories and disturbing thoughts about the victims I had dealt with over the years and I just didn't know what to do about it.

When I was out in Phuket, thousands of pictures of the missing were and were continuing to be posted, in desperation, onto the walls of the mortuary sites every single day. These pictures literally covered the outer walls. I walked past them daily but I could not look at them. I knew they were there, and I knew and understood why, and I will never forget it. But I could not at that time risk stopping, looking and absorbing the humanity of the disaster.

The problem is however, that things like that don't stop happening; they don't go away. A year after the Tsunami there was a TV documentary. Against my better judgement I watched it. They interviewed a man and his children who had lost their mother out in Thailand. I knew her. I had been involved with her identification process at Fulham. You've never seen a bloke move so fast to get hold of the TV remote to switch the television off. The same thing had happened to me with Dunkeswick, when I put on the news and watched the reports about the people who had died in the crash. You would have thought I'd know better by now. But unfortunately, the human interest in disaster is in me, just as it is in the majority of us, and so these programmes pull me in like powerful magnets. And I know now that there's a part of me that I have been repressing all these years that desperately *wants* to establish a human connection to the disasters.

One of the problems I had post-deployment to Thailand, was not having seen the operation through to the end. I knew that this was impossible, due to the enormity of the task but even so, appreciating reality and applying it to oneself are two different things. All of my previous deployments had been neatly 'tied-off' and fully completed. Thailand still felt 'open'. Once I was back home, I constantly followed the news for further identifications. This was nearly impossible from over 7,000 miles away, but close contact with other colleagues who were being deployed in Thailand did provide me with snippets of useful information. I was particularly interested as to whether all the deceased would be identified. With this kind of disaster, it would be unrealistic to believe that all recovered victims would be identified but I was repeatedly asking myself the question: "What happens to the unidentified?' 'What happens to the bodies?"

It was in the spring of 2006, just as the investigation was being scaled down, when I learned that 370 victims remained unidentified in Thailand alone. The majority of these victims were South East Asian. I have spoken previously about the need to obtain scientific post-mortem evidence from a body. Despite some difficulties due to the state of the victim, this usually can be achieved through either a DNA profile from a suitable sample, dental charting and/or fingerprint impressions. Any one or combination of the three will usually provide a very good post-mortem profile of the deceased. But if there is no ante-mortem data for a victim, it is highly unlikely that they will be identified. A sample is always needed from a missing person for comparison against all deceased profiles and records. This ante-mortem information can come in the form of DNA from a close relative or DNA harvested from a personal effect, such as a toothbrush or hairbrush, or from a DNA database if a sample has previously been recorded. The information can also come from ante-mortem dental records or comparison of fingerprints from either a database (if their fingerprint impressions have previously been recorded), or via fingerprint impressions found on the deceased's personal effects at home. If a body is recovered then we always have a chance to create the post-mortem identification profile, but we need to have access to similar profiles of missing persons in order to carry out the ante and post-mortem comparisons. If the deceased person has not been reported missing, then there will not be an opportunity to harvest such vital evidence, meaning that the person will never be identified.

It is my view, that the unidentified persons in this disaster have remained so due to the fact that no one reported them missing, which has resulted in the lack of ante-mortem evidence. It is believed many of these deceased are either Thai or migrant workers from Myanmar. DNA profiles are still held in Bangkok for each of the unidentified deceased victims from the Tsunami, but as they have probably not been reported missing or if they have, then the authorities have not been able to obtain the necessary ante-mortem information and/or profiles required to make the comparisons which leaves a dilemma for the host country of any disaster on a scale such as this; the bodies lie in that country and cannot be repatriated anywhere as they are 'unidentified'. So what are they to do?

The problem was solved by the Thais in 2006 when they built a cemetery at a place called Bang Muang, which is close to the Site 1 mortuary at Wat Yan Yao, about two kilometres from the beach. Here, all the unidentified bodies from the Tsunami in Thailand were buried in individual graves. They have a small concrete headstone, which bears the victim number that had been allocated to them during the post-mortem investigation. Clearly, the religious beliefs of each person could not be taken into account, as their identity was unknown and it would be more disrespectful to make assumptions of their faith in dealing with their laying to rest. Therefore all victims were buried in a dignified manner with the hope that if, in the future, any evidence comes to light which may assist with the identification of any of the unknown victims, then the authorities could consider the new information and match it against the post-mortem records held. If a positive identification is confirmed then the victim can be repatriated to the family.

I was pleased that the Thais built this cemetery; it was a really good decision because even now, it offers a chance and a hope that the number of unidentified victims may decrease. I was intrigued to see the cemetery for myself, so in early 2007, Karon and I took a trip to Thailand.

It was a typical, hot and dry February day when the taxi turned off the main road into the entrance of Wat Yan Yao, the former Site 1 mortuary. I didn't recognise it at first. It was a Buddhist temple once again, guarded by a white perimeter wall and an elaborate gold and red archway, and serenity reigned. The taxi driver stopped exactly where the body storage area once was. As I got out of the vehicle there was no evidence of what had been there before. But what I did get instantly was the smell of death; that horrible stench that consumed me when I first arrived at this site. Adrenaline started to pump as the emotions came crashing back. Karon saw my confused expression and asked what was wrong.

"Can't you smell it?"

"What?"

"The stench!"

My sub-conscious had dragged up something which had obviously lain dormant within me and which my return to this location had triggered with such force that it had brought that rancid stench of death right back to life. It was a bizarre, surreal, experience. It was as though I was straight back in that environment of two years ago. It had never happened to me before – or again since- but I was absolutely convinced that the smell was real. The taxi driver corroborated that I was experiencing a fantasy and laughed. Karon and I both politely returned the laughter but for me this had been a traumatic ordeal; a stark reminder of how grim things had once been there.

Karon sniffed the air. "I can smell jasmine."

Then I noticed the birds were singing. I breathed in. Jasmine. Ok. I looked around and took in the serenity. We stayed at Wat Yan Yao for about fifteen minutes before moving on, driving back south for a few minutes then turning left onto a side road. Within a couple of hundred metres I saw the cemetery at Bang Munag.

Flanked by a white perimeter wall and ornate gates fit for the entry to a King's palace, the cemetery bore a silver plaque about eight feet square on the wall at the side of the entrance. It detailed the flags and names of all 39 countries that had lost nationals in the Tsunami. Seeing that was incredibly moving. Here I was, back in this wonderful country, without any duties or responsibilities and to see the dignified response in dealing with the deceased in the form of this cemetery was hugely gratifying. The taxi driver said that entry was allowed, it was a public place, just like any cemetery in the UK. I swallowed hard as we got out of the taxi and walked through the gates. All I could smell here was jasmine. It was really peaceful. For the first time in Thailand I heard the birds singing to one another. How fitting was this? It was truly beautiful and quite uplifting.

The entrance was a paved walkway about forty metres in length, with a number of stone engravings flanking either side. Positioned in the centre of the walkway was a large granite monument, about thirty feet high. It was shaped like a giant wave; the Tsunami. My adrenalin was pumping. I could feel the tension mounting in my body. A couple of years ago I had gone into a disaster zone with over 8,000 bodies and a tough challenge ahead of me. Today, there was no pressure whatsoever, I was merely a visitor, but in some ways this was even more difficult. Bang Munag reminded me of a military cemetery, full of dignity and as serene as could be. The graves, which had been dug only a few weeks previously, were all ordered regimental style. Rows upon rows of small headstones, each bearing the victims' DVI number. How reassuring it was to see the lengths the Thai authorities had gone to in maintaining dignity (and, speaking as a professional, continuity), even to the grave. The scale of the tragedy hit home again. Here, not a body in sight, but it conjured up images of my visit to Site 1a, seeing all those bodies lying in rows, side-by-side. On this day, I was just a tourist, but I knew I had needed to come, to see this and to tell myself that for me, this was closure.

I remember Karon noticing that I was different. I was quiet, very pensive and quite sullen. That's not me at all, so she said to me that she would go back to the taxi and allow me a few minutes on my own. I am glad she did that. She knows me so well. Karon has made me a different, happier person. Jen has recently remarried and whilst we don't speak anymore, I hope she finds happiness because we were never truly happy. We were married so incredibly young and perhaps, thanks to the direction in which my policing career went, we were doomed to fail.

I took the time to stand and survey the cemetery. I didn't get upset. Far from it. I reflected back to the efforts of the all the DVI teams and the hospitality of the Thai people. I felt a sense of achievement, a sense of worth. I was proud to have been associated with this operation, even if we hadn't identified everyone. I am not aware of any subsequent identifications but hope that these will come. Of the almost 8,500 people who died in Thailand in this disaster, almost 5,500 victims were recovered, half of whom were foreign tourists. The remaining 3,000 people are still missing, presumably consumed by the sea. Statistics are not always reliable on events on this scale, but of the 151 UK victims, all but six were recovered and identified. I spent about five or six minutes with these unknown victims and then suddenly, I felt as if I was able to say goodbye to them, almost as if I'd received their blessing, that it was ok; I wasn't needed anymore. *They didn't need me.* I could move on. I returned to the taxi and smiled warmly at Karon. I was back.

I look back on the Tsunami as a life-enriching experience and feel very privileged to have been part of it. The people I met were amazing, the camaraderie was incredible, especially given the trying circumstances in which we were working, and the learning I gained was invaluable. When you reach the age of 47 you don't expect such opportunities to come along and you certainly don't expect that anything can develop you further, to build on your character any further or to discover character traits that you never knew you had; it certainly exposed some weaknesses in me and the need to admit to myself that in some things I'm not as good as I think I am and I'm certainly not above and beyond being overwhelmed by emotion. I'm not talking about the huge number of victims or the scale of what I saw necessarily, it was more about the isolation, the isolation I'd often felt during my career, during disasters, when – although surrounded by outstanding colleagues – I felt alone and hadn't been able to share my emotions with my friends and family, simply because it wouldn't be fair to them. That was something that had been missing, and it was this I was determined to work on now, to spend time with those I loved the most.

One of the truly great things about my time in Thailand had been the friendliness and warmth shown to me by the Thai people, which fuelled my love for the country and its inhabitants. Karon and I go to Thailand at least once a year. It's impossible not to love a country whose people soldiered on in the face of major adversity and of mass loss of life; both of their own people and of visitors. How they managed to smile and be so warm and welcoming was amazing. The Thais are very special people and will remain dear to my heart forever.

Late in 2005 I got a call from my friend Gill Williams, a Sergeant at Thames Valley Police who had worked in Thailand on DVI. She talked about giving something back to the Thai people, of forming a charity with a DVI colleague of hers from Australia. The purpose of the charity would be to provide an orphanage for the affected area of Thailand. She said they were trying to raise £112,000 in funding and I happily agreed to help. I supported others, staged my own fundraising events and began to donate some of my earnings to the charity. This only seemed right in view of the fact that an element of the training that I was then delivering focused on the Tsunami, its victims and the learning I had been afforded due to their misfortunes. I desperately wanted to give something back to the communities in Phuket. Gill did a fantastic job and with lots of help the charity raised the money. The orphanage opened in 2006. It has two blocks and accommodates 64 boys and girls. The charity is still running and is called Hands Across the Water. Though now retired, Gill still works tirelessly for the orphans. She is one in a million and I have been proud to be associated with her and this excellent cause. I visit every year, bringing gifts and on one occasion, I couldn't help but think of the woman who read my tarot cards all those years ago.

I was in my fifties and death had gone from life, to be replaced by many children. Apart from my involvement in the orphanage, I now have ten grandchildren (with the promise of more to come) so I although I don't believe in the tarot cards, or anything based on superstition; I have to admit that she was right.

On a recent trip to the orphanage I delivered some Christmas presents and the children sang Christmas songs. It was, for me, a moment of pure happiness. I had never thought it possible but life had returned to normal in Thailand. Birds were singing, children were laughing and I couldn't ask for more than that.

ACKNOWLEDGMENTS

That this book exists at all is thanks to my good friend Sandie Higginbotham who, persistent to the last, insisted that I had a story to tell. Thank you Sandie, for your encouragement and your help in getting my story onto the page.

My family have encouraged me throughout the writing of this book, but none more so than my wife, Karon, who has given me her total support and understanding from the day I met her (and whose computer skills saved me on more than one occasion).

Thanks are also due to Kris Hollington, who assisted tremendously with the writing and whose enthusiasm and dedication knows no bounds. My gratitude also goes out to Andrew Lownie, literary agent extraordinaire, whose experience, optimism and tenacity have proven invaluable.

I underestimated just how high and low the emotional rollercoaster would take me as I revisited my past. Tears have been shed, but comfort came from memories of comradeship that got me through some of the darkest times. To my many colleagues, the courageous and honourable men and women who have stood by me, who have worked miracles in impossible conditions and who have lived up to the key principals of Disaster Victim Identification, I thank you from the bottom of my heart.

BIBLIOGRAPHY

A number of reference books proved invaluable when checking procedures, data and outcomes, including:

Bosnia's Million Bones: Solving the World's Greatest Forensic Puzzle, by Christian Jennings (Palgrave Macmillan, 26 Nov 2013)

Disaster Victim Identification: The Practitioner's Guide, edited by Black, Walker, Hackman, Brooks (Dundee University Press, 2010) (and to which I contributed)

Disaster Victim Identification: Experience and Practice, edited by Black, Sunderland, Hackman and Mallett (CRC Press, 17 Jun 2011)

Collective Conviction: The Story of Disaster Action by Anne Eyre and Pam Dix (Liverpool University Press, 30 Sept 2014)

Have an original story you want to tell? Then get in touch. Email info@thistlepublishing.co.uk, with 'Kris Hollington' as the subject heading

Lightning Source UK Ltd.
Milton Keynes UK
UKOW02f0834011016

284245UK00003B/49/P

9 781910 670910